Pick-Up
TRUCKS

Pick-Up TRUCKS

ROB LEICESTER WAGNER

MetroBooks

MetroBooks

An Imprint of Friedman/Fairfax Publishers

Library of Congress Cataloging-in-Publication Data

Wagner, Rob.
    Pick-ups / by Rob Leicester Wagner.
        p.   cm.
    Includes bibliographical references and index.
    ISBN 1-56799-616-7
    1. Trucks—Pictorial works. I. Title.
TL230.12.W34   1998
629.223'2—dc21   97-37165

Editors: Tony Burgess and Ann Kirby
Art Director: Kevin Ullrich
Designer: Robert Allen
Photography Editor: Deidra Gorgos
Production Manager: Jeanne E. Hutter

Printed in China by Leefung-Asco Printers Ltd

10 9 8 7 6 5 4 3 2 1

For bulk purchases and special sales, please contact:
Friedman/Fairfax Publishers
Attention: Sales Department
15 West 26th Street
New York, NY 10010
212/685-6610 FAX 212/685-1307

Visit our website:
http://www.metrobooks.com

DEDICATION

For my wife, Deniece, who knows something about old trucks.

ACKNOWLEDGMENTS

I thank Richard Gray, for sharing his knowledge of the El Camino with me;

Marc Jacoby, for taking me out onto the Los Angeles freeways in his 1957 Chevrolet Cameo;

and Dwight Alexander, for helping me research the toy market.

CONTENTS

Several years ago I had the bright idea of purchasing an old pick-up truck in original but pristine condition and using it as a camper. I wanted a truck and camper that was more distinct and original than the usual roadway fare.

I settled on a 1958 ¾-ton (681kg) Studebaker truck with an 8-foot (2.4m) bed. The next move would be to scout around for an 8-foot (2.4m) camper, and then my dream truck would be set.

The reality of owning an old truck quickly reared its ugly head during those first few months of ownership. I dis-

A white and tan customized Willys is a head-turner at custom and hot rod shows.

Impala while my dad and I delivered Sunday newspapers in the dead of night in my hometown of Sierra Madre, California. Still, my long-distance driving experience came in a '68 International Travelall. The appreciation for getting behind the wheel of a big truck began there.

That's why I bought the Studebaker. I've owned the thing for more than ten years now. I flirted once with selling it, but I couldn't bring myself to do the deed. Besides, my wife told me that with the amount of money I invested in it over the years, I damn well better own it until the day I die.

Those camping trips? Once, to Baja, California. Actual labor duties? I haul the family Christmas tree home in it every year and I once helped a friend move her furniture with it. The truck turned out to be my weekend driver.

I've managed to forgive myself (although my wife hasn't) for buying a truck that is now forty years old with my heart and not my head. But that's the whole point, isn't it? Most folks don't need a pick-up truck, yet 6 million new light-duty trucks were sold last year. That's one pick-up truck for every 2.6 cars. Or, as *Car and Driver* magazine put it: "For every wonderful Audi A4 sedan sold in the U.S., Ford sells eighty F-Series pick-ups." Clearly this vehicle has caught the American fancy.

covered the drum brakes were not practical for today's city driving. I missed certain creature comforts of modern trucks, such as not having engine heat billowing into the cab during the summer and sending interior temperatures into three digits. Still, I had made my bed, and I was determined to lie in it.

Owning a truck had never before been a top priority during my driving life. I cut my driving teeth on a '59 Chevy

Until the late 1970s, the pick-up truck was relegated to workhorse status. That changed in 1978, when 4 million pick-ups were sold. It was clear even two decades ago that the light-duty pick-up truck had become a status symbol of sorts. It has slowly replaced the '49 Merc, the '67 Ford Mustang, and the '71 Plymouth Barracuda as the teen-rebel, terrorizing machine of the road.

The light truck also has gained celebrity status in recent years. Check out some of these famous people and their babies: rock musicians Eddie Van Halen (Chevy 1500 with customized "5150" graphics from his record album) and Sammy Hagar (a late '40s Chevy), football quarterback Troy Aikman (GMC pick-up), comedian Tim Allen (GMC pick-up), basketball player and flavor of the month Dennis Rodman (Ford F-150 SuperCab 4X4), and Electronic Data Systems CEO Les Alberthal (Chevy C/K).

These guys buy their vehicles like the average Joe: with their hearts.

In the span of a generation, the nation's truck drivers have turned from a homogenized, well-ordered cross section of rural life into rebels with questionable cause. It's refreshing to make a statement by rejecting the glitz and glamour of a Mercedes-Benz, BMW, or Audi in favor of an edgy attitude and a reminder of the great and rugged outdoors. Pick-up trucks, and especially sport utility vehicles, have filled that bill—even if parking lots are now filled with pick-up trucks and sport utility vehicles that blur the line between fashion statement and individuality.

While most urban truck owners these days hardly consider such things, there is a practical view to owning a pick-up. Trucks have a long history of outlasting their passenger-car counterparts. The average age of a pick-up is around fifteen years, compared to only a ten-year life for passenger cars. And it's conceivable that the life span of a pick-up truck will increase over the next decade with the introduction of the radically designed Dodge Ram and the new Ford F-150, which offered a rough-and-tumble truck for the personal-use driver who is looking for something sleek and aerodynamic, something that isn't just a plain ol' car.

The trend toward this type of consumer interest became truly evident when Ford sold 698,418 full-size F-Series trucks in 1996. That's only 45,190 fewer vehicles sold than the

Custom truck owners can get inventive—this 1947 Ford has been chopped into a convertible and fitted with a 1938 nose.

combined sales of the Ford Taurus and Honda Accord. Dodge Ram sales figures are nothing short of mind-boggling. Before the restyling effort, Dodge sold 95,542 full-size Ram pick-ups. In 1994, the first full year of the new truck, 232,092 Rams were sold. The Dodge Dakota, three-quarters the size of the Ram, is also expected to see skyrocketing sales. Dodge's Ram-style sport utility vehicle, the Durango, could very well put Dodge over the top in sales for the first time in the truck maker's history.

Purists may argue today that truck builders have gone to the extreme to coddle today's consumer with a kinder, gentler kind of truck. Cloth or even leather seats, cup holders, CD players, consoles for change, and plastic everywhere have definitely turned off some longtime truck lovers who long for the simpler pleasures of the classic pick-up.

I confess that I fall into the category of the old-school truck jockey who prefers the cold steel dashboard and an AM radio to the soft dash and quad-speaker stereo of today's models. But why be selfish? Ford and Dodge have the right idea to expand the market beyond the limited adult male market and cash in by attracting teenagers and female drivers. Whether or not the farmer goes the way of the milkman, there will always be a reason to buy what has become a true American icon, the pick-up truck. And it'll usually be bought with the heart.

Perhaps no other truck built in the United States has endured like Ford's F-Series trucks. Since the 1948 debut of the F-1 "Bonus Built" pick-ups and the revolutionary F-100 Anniversary truck, Ford and its F-150 Series have dominated the light-duty pick-up market.

Ford traces the lineage of its trucks much further back than 1948, of course. The Model E delivery wagon debuted in 1904, only one year after Henry Ford founded the Ford Motor Company, and was produced until 1911. By then the Model T passenger car had been in full production for three years.

The Model E's replacement, the now legendary Model T truck, featured a 20-horsepower, four-cylinder engine and planetary transmission. It rode on $4^3/_4$- by 19-inch (12 by 48cm) hard-rubber truck tires and came equipped with cowl-mounted acetylene headlamps, although early models came with no windshield. With the addition of electric lights, pneumatic tires, and a windshield, sales of the Model T truck soared. More than 1 million trucks were sold before the Model T was phased out in 1927.

ABOVE: Hood ornament from a 1936 Ford V-8 pick-up.
OPPOSITE: Delivery trucks such as this 1925 Ford were ubiquitous on the road in 1920s America. But the design was outdated, even for 1925, compared with more streamlined Chevrolets produced that year. The cab and rear portion of the truck are constructed of wood.

The Model T passenger car and, later, the truck enjoyed an extraordinary life span. As Henry Ford perfected the assembly line, the cost of a Model T car dropped from between $800 and $1,000 per unit to less than $300 in the mid-1920s. It was a well-built vehicle, but lacked panache and personality. Still, Ford saw no reason to fix something that wasn't broken.

Henry Ford's son Edsel thought otherwise. A tragic visionary who died in 1943, perhaps before realizing his full potential, Edsel is largely thought of as a man who, had he only worked independently of his father, might have achieved the greatness of automobile luminaries such as William Durant, Alfred P. Sloan Jr., Harley Earl, Virgil Exner, Ed Cole, and Harlow "Red" Curtice.

While no match for his father's strong personality and ego—and thus relegated to the shadows of the Ford Motor Company—Edsel had worked quietly and diligently to bring prestige and engineering greatness to the Lincoln. In the mid-1920s, flush with the success of the Lincoln, Edsel turned his

ABOVE: A four-cylinder Ford Huckster engine. **LEFT:** Edsel Ford's influence greatly changed the styling of the Ford Model A; this is a 1930 model. Sales soared after the debut of the Model A in 1928. Subtle changes ordered by Ford made a dramatic difference in the overall appearance of the vehicle.

attention to the Model T. In 1926, even with new car registrations hovering at 200,163 to Chevrolet's paltry 55,623, Edsel sensed that buyers were bored with the Model T's design. Reliability and simple workmanship could only go so far.

Just as Edsel predicted, Chevrolet surged ahead in new truck registrations in 1927, with 104,832 to Ford's 99,451. And Edsel anticipated that Chevrolet would outstrip Ford in sales again for 1928.

Lobbying his father, Edsel advocated retiring the Model T for an updated version. After much wrangling, Henry Ford discontinued Model T production on May 25, 1927. Model A production began on December 2, 1927.

The Model A was a masterpiece. Its design was really not much different than that of its predecessor, but the subtle changes made it feel like a new creation. Its simple, free-flowing lines were graceful in execution, and its reliable four-cylinder engine was boosted to 200 cubic inches with a three-speed transmission and a 1½-ton (1,362kg) carrying capacity. Ultimately, Ford's revolutionary Model A was simply the Model T perfected after years of benign neglect.

Buyers immediately recognized its carrying potential and put larger pneumatic tires on it to increase its payload. While

OPPOSITE: The chrome front bumper dips at the center to give the '36 pick-up a fluid motion and complement the grille. The windshield is equipped with only one wiper, but sports a passenger-side rearview mirror.

the Model A was introduced too late in 1928 to lift the balance ledger for that year—the Model A had only 65,247 new registrations for 1928 compared with Chevrolet's 133,682—the next year proved its clout. In 1930, during the first full year of the Great Depression, Ford recorded 197,216 new truck registrations as opposed to Chevy's 118,253.

In 1932 Ford introduced the V-8 engine, stunning the car and truck industry. It came equipped with either a 60- or 80-horsepower engine and was complemented by a new four-speed transmission. Only two years later the Ford truck featured pontoon fenders integrated into the running boards and a simple, vertical grille with vertical louvers on the hood.

The year 1934 was pivotal for the truck maker. While its total new truck registrations lagged behind Chevrolet by nearly 30,000 units, Ford scratched its way into a heated battle with its rival. Buyers took notice of the V-8 with its strong power, good fuel economy, and reduced oil consumption. To sweeten the package, the standard equipment was upgraded and more options were made available.

ABOVE: This 1936 Ford ½-ton pick-up sports a V-8 engine, which revolutionized engine technology in the 1930s.
RIGHT: The instrument cluster of a 1936 Ford pickup truck.

OVERLEAF: This 1940 Ford ½-ton pick-up reflects industrial design elements of the late 1930s and early 1940s. The rear chrome bumper is an option, probably an after-market item. Wide whitewall tires also are an option and were certainly uncommon when the truck was new. Also note the overall absence of chrome.

Perhaps the most popular pick-up during the 1930s was the Model 46, one of Ford's lowest-priced offerings. Closed-cab versions sold for about $470 and featured options such as chrome-plated bumpers, graphite shackle bushings, and re-styled hubcaps. Even in those early days, Ford liked to brag of its V-8 engine. Hoods were equipped with the telltale blue Ford emblem with a V-8 logo below it.

The new pick-up models for 1935 showed the first signs of a new industry trend. Much like rival Chevrolet, Ford began to phase out its mimicking of passenger-car styling, and instead featured its own exclusive heavy-duty truck design. The changes, such as chrome louvers and bumpers, were largely cosmetic at first. The ½-ton Model 50 (454kg) pick-up with 112-inch (284.5cm) wheelbase and the 1½-ton (1,362kg) Model 51 with standard steel cab and 131½-inch (334cm) wheelbase also gained in popularity. These trucks were equipped with 221-ci V-8s that generated 80 horsepower at 3800 rpm.

Ford continued with more significant model changes for 1937, such as the Model 83 with its 112-inch (284.5cm) wheelbase and powerful V-8s rated variously at 60, 85, 95, and 100 horsepower. More importantly, 1938 witnessed the debut of the very attractive and now-classic egg-shaped grille.

Ford took time out from building trucks during World War II to build B-24 bombers at its River Rouge plant near Detroit. After the war ended in 1946, the company returned to commercial truck manufacturing but, like its rivals, Ford continued to rely on prewar designs. That changed for the 1948 model year with the debut of the venerable F-Series light-duty pick-up.

The postwar popularity of the 1948–52 "Bonus Built" pick-up has been obscured somewhat by the 1953 model year introduction of the F-100 Ford Anniversary pick-up, now considered the watershed model for the truck maker. Still, during that four-year period, Ford produced 841,000 F-Series trucks to capture an average of a little more than 20 percent of each year's market. In 1950 alone, 345,801 Ford trucks were sold to buyers, accounting for a 25.2 percent share of the market and a whopping 70.3 percent of all light trucks sold under 10,000 GVW (gross vehicle weight).

The F-1 was introduced by Ford brass on January 18, 1948, as the first completely redesigned truck since the 1938 model. Its moniker, "Bonus Built," was meant to imply that the customer was getting something a little extra for his or her money. With all-new sheet metal, a single-piece windshield, and vent windows, this was a truck that wouldn't let the buyer down. The fenders and hood were squared and the cab measured 3 inches (7.5cm) taller, 7 inches (18cm) wider, and 3 inches (7.5cm) longer than the prewar models. Chrome was still rare in the years immediately following the war, so painted argent silver graced the new recessed grille.

Even the instrument panel had been newly redesigned, with a pod to the right of the driver containing the speedometer and a separate pod on the left displaying the temperature, battery, fuel, and oil gauges. Intended for a strictly male market, it even featured an optional cigar lighter.

The truck line started with an F-1 designation for the ½-ton (454kg) model all the way up to F-7 and F-8 for the 3-ton (2,724kg) versions.

Despite the stunning redesign of the F-Series truck, total Ford truck registrations in 1949 nose-dived to 202,179, while Chevrolet enjoyed a banner year of 345,519 new truck registrations. Desperate to keep the public interested in its trucks, Ford brass introduced the Five Star cab and the Five Star Extra cab in 1951. These options featured such extras as three-way ventilation, an adjustable seat, and two-tone color paint schemes. There was also a driver's side visor, a dispatch box, dual windshield wipers, and an ashtray. The seats were stuffed with additional foam padding for comfort, and extra sound-deadening material was installed in the floor, doors, and rear portion of the cab panel. Also new for the '51 model year was the name "FORD" spelled out on the upper grille panel. A new 239-cubic-inch V-8, generating 106 horsepower at 3500 rpm, was introduced for 1951 and included a new fan and bell housing, manifolds, generator, and carburetor to complement the new F-Series look.

The truck kept its basic design for 1952, although the grille was changed to a heavier, single massive horizontal bar supported by three vertical ones. The standard engine, aside from the 239-ci version, was the 215-ci V-8 that developed 101 horsepower at 3500 rpm. The F-1 was placed on a 114-inch (289.5cm) wheelbase with an overall length of 188 inches (477.5cm) and an overall width of 75.9 inches (193cm).

Much of the appreciation for the accomplishments in design and engineering of the "Bonus Built" trucks was lost—or at least forgotten—when Ford sought dramatic styling changes in the new F-100 pick-up in 1953. To celebrate its fiftieth anniversary, Ford was determined to give light-truck buyers an easier and more stylish ride.

L.D. Crusoe, vice president of Ford, told automotive writers that Ford had invested $50 million in research, development, engineering, and testing to come up with a new light-duty pick-up concept. The result was a truck with a tall cab, a

Completely stocked and restored to its original appearance, this 1950 F-1 offers wide whitewall tires and wood stakes in the bed.

LEFT: Coming off the popular F-1 Series was the 1953 Ford F-100 model that again set the standard for truck design. Millions of dollars were invested in research to produce a truck to celebrate Ford's fiftieth anniversary. Sales for the first year outstripped both Chevrolet and Dodge.

smartly angled, curved windshield, and a two-bar grille flanking a handsome V-8 or three-pointed star emblem. The hood now featured a new Ford emblem with the word "FORD" scripted across the top against a black background. Underneath this logo, a lighting bolt slashed through a gear, all against a red background.

The research paid off: 1953 saw the sale of 116,437 F-100s. The rush for these trucks also spurred sales for the F-100's big brothers, the F-250 and F-350 trucks.

Research by Ford also found that truck owners wanted more in comfort and safety. The new curved windshield and 4-foot (1.2m) -wide rear window improved visibility. Deeper door windows allowed the driver to rest an arm comfortably on the sill. Advertisements of the day touted that the 56.7-inch (144cm)-wide bench seat could sit three average-sized men, although today's drivers would probably consider such quarters to be somewhat cramped. Options included such stylish and

RIGHT: The '53 F-100 model featured a 239-cubic-inch V-8 that generated 106 horsepower.

ABOVE: Ford V-8 from the 1965 model. LEFT: Clean lines and no-nonsense styling characterize this 1965 Ford ¹/₂-ton model. A high percentage of '60s Fords remain on the road today, not only as show vehicles but as workhorses.

comfortable additions as two-tone upholstery, foam rubber seat cushions, a chrome grille, and stainless steel trim around the windshield and rear window.

The dashboard was spartan, even for a truck. An instrument pod clustered the speedometer and other gauges directly in front of the driver. The rest of the dash was virtually bare as it swept across to the passenger side.

The box measured 6¹/₂ feet (2m) and was decorated with seasoned wood protected by steel strips. A stamped "FORD" on the tailgate replaced the traditional script logo used for many years.

The 1953 model offered two engines: the standard 215-ci, six-cylinder engine that developed 101 horsepower—dubbed the Cost Clipper—and the 239-ci, 106-horsepower V-8. Ford's marketing team crowed about the 1953 model's "greatest transmission choice in truck history." The Fordomatic transmission was available on ¹/₂-ton (454kg) models for the first time, proving that the company was committed to driver comfort. The manual transmission selections included the standard three- and four-speed SynchroSilent units. A three-speed transmission with overdrive was also available. Even the turning radius for the '53 models was reduced by 14 percent to give the truck slightly better handling in tight quarters.

With the freshly redesigned 1997 F-150, Ford anticipates sales to reach 700,000 units per year. Pick-up truck purists, especially those not particularly loyal to Ford, have pooh-poohed the '97 F-150 as bowing to the pressures of passenger-car comfort and looks, such as the gentle curves that are 6 percent more aerodynamic than the previous year's offerings. Still, whatever the Ford marketing strategists lost in testosterone-fueled cowboy trucks of the past, they more than recovered in new customers with the '97 model. In 1995 women made up 10 percent of the full-size pick-up truck market. That number hit 20 percent with the introduction of the 1997 truck models, thanks in no small part to Ford.

Ford has taken several other steps toward attracting more women buyers. Optional running boards, for example, cut down the gigantic distance between ground and cab. Ford marketed this as helpful to women in skirts as they climb into the cab, but in reality it made entry easier for most people.

Under the new sloped hood of the '97 F-150, the buyer has the option of a base 4.2-liter V-6 engine that generates 205 horsepower at 4400 rpm or the 4.6-liter V-8 with 210 horsepower at 4400 rpm.

While Chevrolet for years has taken top-dog honors in overall truck sales, the Ford F-1, F-100, and F-150 light-duty trucks have by far outstripped every other truck maker in total sales and popularity. The three models are widely perceived as icons of durability and rugged individualism.

By 1956 the F-100 sold for a base price of $1,521 and featured a bigger 272-ci V-8 engine generating 167 horsepower at 4400 rpm with a two-barrel Holley carburetor and an 8:1 compression ratio. Sitting on a 110-inch (279.5cm) wheelbase, its overall length was 189 inches (480cm), and it measured 75½ inches (192cm) in height and 75.7 inches (192.5cm) in width.

The popularity of the F-Series trucks over the next decade or so ebbed and flowed. In recent years, however, the line has again become the most popular truck among buyers, with the Chevrolet C/K Series coming in a wheezing, distant second place. In another light, the F-150 has been America's best-selling vehicle—that's any vehicle—for more than a decade. Forty percent more F-150s are produced annually than the country's best-selling passenger car, the Ford Taurus.

In 1995 about 691,000 full-size F-Series trucks were sold. By comparison, Chevrolet's C/K Series sold only 537,000 units. In 1996 total F-Series sales topped 22.5 million, demolishing the previous record set by the Volkswagen beetle.

ABOVE: Ford's smaller trucks, like this mid-size 1993 Ranger XL, fared better than the Dodge Dakotas in the early 1990s. The horizontal and vertical bars serving as the grille and the soft, rounded look of the front fenders, hood, and bumper remain a consistent theme in all Ford truck products. **RIGHT:** The third door of the extended-cab 1997 Ford F-150 allows easy access for passengers and cargo. **OPPOSITE:** A simpler, less masculine mesh grille exemplifies Ford's desire for a softer look.

RESTORATION

The restoration of light-duty pick-up trucks is a fairly recent phenomenon. As late as the 1970s and early 1980s, many Ford F-100s and Chevrolet Apaches were still tooling the roads as workhorses. Fifteen or twenty years ago, refurbishing old trucks bordered on the ludicrous; the investment required to restore them would have exceeded the truck's actual value by as much as ten times.

By the late '80s, however, that had changed dramatically. For one thing, the infrastructure of the restoration business had developed, which lowered costs. Indeed, automobile restoration was peaking as a multibillion-dollar industry.

Fully restored, one-hundred-point Duesenbergs, Stutzes, Cadillacs, and Bentleys were commanding six-figure prices. The Japanese purchased '50s American cars by the gross at exorbitant prices and shipped them overseas. The average car enthusiast was forced to focus his or her attention on more affordable cars: '50s Chevrolets, Fords, and Chryslers, or perhaps the '60s muscle and pony cars.

When recession hit in the early 1990s, collector-car prices dropped sharply before stabilizing. Now, a fully restored 1957 Ford Thunderbird no longer commands $40,000 but $25,000.

Enthusiasts hungered for projects that didn't require a second mortgage on the house. Aggressive truck clubs such as the American Truck Historical Society, dedicated to preserving truck history, helped fill this need. They speed the natural progression of a market based on refurbishing the light-duty pick-up truck. For example, a Model A Ford pick-up may require up to twelve hun-

dred man-hours at $45 an hour for a complete restoration. A '55 Chevy Bel Air convertible, by contrast, may require up to twenty-eight hundred man-hours.

Still, remember that while restoring a forty-year-old truck may not be as expensive or complicated as rebuilding a 1957 Plymouth Fury, it can also cost a pretty penny. The difference in investment is wide, but so is the gap in expected return. A California man paid $70,000 in 1994 to fully restore his 1956 Ford F-100. Top value today? About $8,500, perhaps $10,000 for the right buyer.

The key to restoring an old vehicle, especially a collectible truck, comes through properly gauging the depth of one's pocketbook and determining one's wants and needs. The auto/truck restoration industry basically relies on three levels of restoration: a full body-off-frame disassembly, a partial restoration, or a cosmetic restoration. It is important to understand the distinction among the three. Classified advertisements are littered with cars and trucks touted as fully restored. Buyers often find out—too late—that such vehicles are less than what is advertised.

The true meaning of restoration is a frame-off operation, that is, the body is removed from the frame and virtually every part is disassembled and restored to its original condition, if not better than when it rolled off the assembly line. The frame is dip-stripped or sandblasted; the leaf springs are disassembled, cleaned, and then re-arched; and the coil springs are replaced. The brake system is rebuilt from scratch, the gas tank removed and boiled out, and the exhaust system replaced.

Correct in every detail, this 1949 Dodge ½-ton pick-up is restored to its original green and black color combination. Note standard white wheels and black tires. No wide whitewalls for this truck.

The engine receives a ground-up rebuild with components replaced as necessary. Wood framing, used in most prewar vehicles, is replaced with new hickory. The list goes on and on, but it's easy to see why thousands of man-hours are required. Neither engine nor body is customized, but rather rebuilt to original factory specifications.

If this is accomplished, then the final product might be called a one-hundred-point concours vehicle. This moniker derives from a common scoring system used by clubs to rate a car or truck. One hundred points is considered a perfect score. Very few trucks, however, need or even deserve such detailed attention from a restorer.

There are many cost-saving alternatives available to the enthusiast. A "fenders-off" restoration serves the average collector quite well. In this process, the front and rear fenders, hood, trunk, doors, instrument

panel, and bed of the truck are removed. The frame and body parts are degreased and refinished, or may be sandblasted and powder-coated to ensure durability. The engine is often rebuilt.

ABOVE: A 1938 Ford stakebed with its trademark egg-shaped grille.
LEFT: The cost of chroming grilles, like on this 1946 Chevrolet canopy truck, often varies depending on the quality of the work.

cles that are used daily or at least frequently. Special attention is paid to bodywork and painting, plating chrome, and engine repair, or perhaps a rebuild of the engine if the budget allows.

At this level of restoration, the collector can enjoy a specific level of control over the restoration of the car or truck as the pocketbook allows. For example, a new wiring harness, new glass, or replating chrome can be added to the project.

The bottom level of restoration applies only to later-model trucks or older vehicles in very good original condition or that have already undergone quality restoration. This type of restorative work is normally applied to vehicles that are "drivers"—vehi-

The restoration of a vehicle is a personal choice, based on one's own expectations and standards. Still, much confusion reigns in the industry. Professional restorers often espouse an interpretation of what is necessary to complete a full restoration that only the rich can afford. Even with the industry's strict interpretation of what exactly is a complete restoration, sellers often don't pay attention to such details, and buyers often lack the knowledge and expertise to determine what is a fully restored vehicle.

The bottom line? It's a buyer-beware market. One must enter the car-restoration field with extreme care or else find oneself taking out the second mortgage if the final product is to be realized. Just remember: no matter what anyone says, mid- or low-level restorations do not require that every piece be replaced. It's the buyer's choice.

A few names cannot be excluded from any discussion of restoration. Samuel E. Bailey of Bala Cynwyd, Pennsylvania, is often considered the father of the field. His restorations of a 1909 Pierce-Arrow and a 1914 Mercer Raceabout were honored by the Antique Automobile Club of America.

If Bailey was the founder of auto/truck restoration, then William F. "Bill" Harrah would be the world's curator of restored cars and trucks. A vehicle enthusiast since he was a boy, Harrah owned a two-cylinder Maxwell Runabout that he believed was a 1907 model. But when he participated in the Horseless Carriage Club tour from Los Angeles to San Diego in 1948, Maxwell lovers noted it was actually a 1911 model and that many mistakes had been made during the restoration process. This led to an obsession by Harrah for accuracy, as he vowed never to make such errors again.

Harrah developed manuals that gave correct technical information and a step-by-step process for the restoration of specific vehicles. Sparks, Nevada, served as his base of operations, in which engine rebuilding, painting, upholstery, electrical systems, and woodworking were given painstaking attention to detail and accuracy. By the 1970s he owned an estimated fifteen hundred old automobiles in various states of repair and original condition.

It was Harrah who set the standard for automobile and truck restoration. But the term "restoration" has always been defined broadly.

The restoration of fender emblems that feature both chrome and different color paint, as seen on this 1948 Chevrolet Apache, should be left to a professional.

CHAPTER TWO

GMC

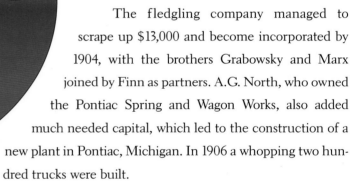

Today's GMC truck is merely a marketing division for Chevrolet and various other General Motors assembly divisions. Identical to the Chevrolet except for powertrain options, model badges, and grille, the GMC truck is a shadow of its former self.

But up until 1970 the GMC truck wielded a formidable reputation as a dependable workhorse for the farmer and small urban hauler. In fact, today's GMC truck continues to ride on the steller reputation it forged in the early 1950s, despite changes in GM's standards for the line.

The GMC truck was the brainchild of Max Grabowsky, who put up his money in 1900, with saloonkeepers Barney Finn and Albert Marx, to give birth to a truck empire. Under the company name of Rapid Motor Vehicle Company, Max and his brother, Morris, developed their first truck in a Detroit garage in 1902 for the American Garment Cleaning Company. The truck had a top speed of 10 miles per hour (16kph). Over the next two years, seventy-five trucks were manufactured, a respectable number given the Grabowskys' limited production facilities.

ABOVE: A GMC emblem on a fender. OPPOSITE: This 1995 GMC Sonoma 4×4 SLE comes equipped with an enhanced Vortec V-6 engine and four-wheel ABS brakes on all models. The Sonoma competes in the same market as the Ford Ranger and the Dodge Dakota.

The fledgling company managed to scrape up $13,000 and become incorporated by 1904, with the brothers Grabowsky and Marx joined by Finn as partners. A.G. North, who owned the Pontiac Spring and Wagon Works, also added much needed capital, which led to the construction of a new plant in Pontiac, Michigan. In 1906 a whopping two hundred trucks were built.

In 1911 Rapid and another company, Reliance Trucks, merged. The new company assumed the moniker General Motors Company, and their trucks soon bore GMC badges. But it wasn't until October 13, 1916, that the company's name was changed to General Motors Corporation.

World War I proved to be a boon to American truck makers. Horses, the traditional choice for transporting materials and supplies, were judged to be too expensive to feed and maintain. For the first time, the U.S. Army employed trucks in their place.

In 1921 the K-Series GMC truck debuted with a self-starter, electric lights, and a power tire pump. The next season's 2-ton (1,816kg) models featured a seven-speed

WHOLESALE
Y-VEAL-BUTTER AND EGGS

LEFT: A 1-ton GMC truck is fitted with solid rear tires, but pneumatic tires in the front. This mid-1920s version typifies the lack of creature comforts on trucks of the era. RIGHT: Some coachbuilders outdid themselves with ornate styling, as evident on this mid-1920s GMC truck. BELOW: Canvas-covered trucks, like this GMC model, were familiar sights on city streets in the 1920s.

transmission assembled by grafting a two-speed gearbox to the back of a four-speed transmission. The resulting device offered a dual-range, twin-stick-shift transmission.

GMC was just one of dozens of truck makers in the United States in the early 1920s. Fortunes were quickly won and lost as just about anybody with a blacksmith shop was capable of producing at least one light-duty truck for sale. But that changed for GMC on August 12, 1925, when it merged with Yellow Cab Manufacturing Company. GM's Alfred P. Sloan Jr. became a coexecutive manager with John D. Hertz to strengthen the company's position in the truck-building industry.

GMC truck sales after the merger climbed dramatically. The year 1926 witnessed the registration of 2,797 new GMCs

ABOVE: This 1937 ½-ton pick-up typifies the clean, industrial look that emerged in the late 1930s. RIGHT: Another view of a 1937 GMC ½-ton pickup. Black fenders were standard.

in the United States. The following year saw that figure more than double to 6,637, then rise to 17,568 by 1928. To accommodate growing production, General Motors committed itself to building an $8 million plant in Pontiac in 1927.

For 1929, total GMC registrations were recorded at 14,300. Production was no doubt clipped in the last two months of the year, following the stock market crash. GMC registrations plummeted from 9,004 in 1930 to 6,919 in 1931; 6,359 in 1932; and 6,602 in 1933. When the Depression hit its lowest depths in 1931, General Motors slashed truck prices by up to $500, but the wrecked economy dragged on into 1932 and 1933. In 1934, the year after President Franklin D. Roosevelt took office, the economy rebounded slightly and total GMC truck registrations climbed to a respectable 10,449. Total truck registrations for the truck maker remained relatively healthy for the rest of the decade, peaking at 43,522 in 1937.

At a modest $595 for a 1¹/₂- to 2-ton (1,362 to 1,816kg) model chassis, GMC's reduced prices surely helped the company move plenty of trucks during those lean years. But, compared with Ford's bargain-priced 1¹/₂-ton (1,362kg) pick-up, sticker priced at $500, GMC's production numbers were still fairly modest.

GMC abandoned the British market shortly after the stock market crash of 1929, but the company returned in 1936. GMC's T14 chassis were popular for 1-ton (908kg) delivery vans, with coachbuilding performed by Forest Gate or Bonallack & Sons of London. The 1938 GMC T16 1¹/₂-ton (1,362kg) models were marketed in England as the Model 3TB 3-ton (2,724kg) model. Among its many features were a graceful chrome front bumper that dipped in the middle, turn signals on top of the fenders, and a single-piece windshield. The front grille was designed in an interesting pattern, with vertical chrome stripes spaced along the nose and three sets of stripes that crossed the length of the nose.

As the economy improved, General Motors opened a truck plant in Oakland, California, in 1937. By 1939 GM began building six-cylinder engines exclusively for trucks. Four-cylinder, two-cycle diesel engines also debuted in 1939. These

ABOVE: This 1936 GMC truck gets a new diesel engine.

particular specifications would later be associated with the popular Detroit diesel line.

During World War II, GMC produced nearly 600,000 military vehicles between December 1941 and August 1945, many of them the amphibian truck DUKW, affectionately labeled the "Duck." Production workers responsible for assembling the craft were honored with the army-navy "E" award, each branch's highest civilian honor.

Steel shortages hindered GMC's immediate postwar production. Less than 26,000 vehicles were built in 1946, and only a modest 49,187 were produced in 1947. These supply problems eased themselves eventually, and 1951 saw total GMC truck registrations hit 100,285.

The year 1948 marked the end of a distinct GMC truck line. That year's model of Advance-Design light-duty truck

LEFT: GMC, like other truck makers, geared up for the war effort, and by 1943 was in full swing. Here, women workers take on the lion's share of the truck assembly tasks by building engines. RIGHT: Factory workers install an engine into a GMC truck.

replicated the previous year's Chevrolet truck of the same name in almost every aspect. The engine, grille, nameplate, and badging retained the GMC label, but otherwise that truck and its successors would be swept along by the designs of other members of the General Motors umbrella.

As the 1950s dawned, GMC focused its attention on improving fuel economy and reducing the amount of required engine maintenance. Under the leadership of Roger M. Keyes, vice president of General Motors and general manager of GMC's truck and coach division, GMC studied the lessons of World War II, when fuel and steel were in short supply. In 1951, at the height of the Korean War, GMC introduced its diesel "Million Miler," available with a three-, four-, or six-cylinder engine. These new engines offered extremely high life expectancies and featured fuel modulators and parts specifically designed to be interchangeable with older GMC engines. The fuel modulator was a self-contained governor assembly to control the amount of fuel injected into the cylinder at speeds below 1600 rpm.

Several new 1½-ton (1,362kg) models debuted in 1950 as horsepower and cubic-inch displacement were stepped up. New engines featured cubic-inch displacements of 228 with horsepower increasing from 94.5 to 96; 248-ci displacements with horsepower boosted from 100 to 110; and the 270-ci displacement with pony power jumping from 104 to 120. Additionally, GMC engineers redesigned the intake manifold, installed new high-lift cams, changed the valve timing, and enlarged the carburetor throat. Despite these changes, the engines remained relatively light and didn't increase fuel consumption significantly for the light- and medium-duty trucks they served.

GMC focused on ways to increase horsepower without rendering existing engines or engine parts obsolete. As before,

Attractive and simple in design, this 1948 GMC pick-up performs mule duties. Note the absence of a rear bumper, but a chrome bumper in front.

strict standards ensured that new parts could be installed on existing engines. The 6-71 engine, for example, featured an aluminum block, cylinder heads, bell housing, and other parts to reduce the weight of various GMC engines by as much as 420 pounds (191kg) from older versions.

The first generation of true postwar truck designs emerged between 1948 and 1953. In 1954 GMC and Chevrolet underwent another radical design change with a single-piece windshield and redesigned grille. To complement these new effects, two-tone paint jobs and color-coordinated interiors were also introduced. Under the hood sat a brand-new 248½-ci, inline six-cylinder engine that offered 125 horsepower. The three-speed transmission could be arrayed on either a floor-mounted or a steering-column–mounted gearshift.

This 1954 model is remembered as a rare instance when the GMC truck retained a small part of its individuality. The dual-range, Hydra-Matic automatic transmission was an option introduced in 1953 for GMC that didn't appear on Chevy trucks until a year later. Furthermore, while the GMC's foundation was Chevrolet, the GMC's widened grille and integrated rectangular parking lights gave it a stockier, lower appearance than its counterpart.

For much of its life through the 1970s, GMC was a virtual clone of Chevrolet. It differentiated itself largely through a variety of pricey optional packages, appealing to more upscale buyers. Then as now there persisted a certain air associated with owning a GMC. This draws upon GMC's old reputation

GMC trucks, like this 1948 150-Series ³/₄-ton pick-up, perform a wide variety of tasks in locations ranging from farms to urban areas.

as a tough taskmaster, compared with the more sedate and rider-friendly Chevrolet.

The identical twin to the Chevrolet C/K pick-up, the GMC Sierra light-duty pick-up has lost none of its edge in its truck roots. The mid-1990s Sierra line included ¹/₂-, ³/₄-, and 1-ton (454, 681, and 908kg) trucks, with models ranging from the regular to extended four-door crew cabs. The Widebox regular bed and Stepside (or Sportside) bed were offered in both the long and short versions.

The 1995 model Sierra featured a completely redesigned dash to be more ergonomically friendly and refined. It also offered a safety device similar to that of the C/K pick-ups with a driver's-side airbag and brake-transmission shift-interlock

ABOVE: GMC engineers test the engine in a 1957 ½-ton pickup truck. LEFT: The GMC 150 was nearly identical to the Chevrolet line with the exception of the grille and other minor alterations.

mechanism. This prevents the truck from being shifted out of park unless the brake is depressed.

Ranging in price from $13,500 to $28,000, the Sierra came equipped with either a 4.3-liter V-6 engine at 165 horsepower or a 6.5-liter V-8 rated to 155, 180, or 190 horsepower. Buyers could choose from three wheelbases: 117½, 131½, or 155½ inches (298.5, 334, or 395cm). Bed spaces measured at either 6½ or 8 feet (2 or 2.4m). Its curbside weight reached 3,829 pounds (1,738kg), with a maximum towing capacity of 13,500 pounds (6,129kg) and a maximum payload capacity of 5,500 pounds (2,497kg).

The GMC Sonoma, which competed against the Chevrolet S-10 and Dodge Dakota, again offered a slightly more refined package, with three trim levels and three engine choices. At the low end of the powertrain labors the 2.2-liter, 100-horsepower, four-cylinder engine, then the 4.3-liter, 165-horsepower V-6 and the 4.3-liter, 195-horsepower version.

LEFT: The newly styled 1954 GMC ½-ton 100-Series trucks sported a two-tone paint scheme, some hood chrome, a new grille, and a single-piece windshield.

BELOW: This 1955 GMC 100-Series Suburban ½-ton pick-up truck was GMC's answer to the Chevrolet Cameo Carrier. It's hard to believe that a truck maker could come up with something fancier than the Cameo, but the limited-edition Suburban was adorned with more chrome on a significantly different grille, and offered a more elaborate dashboard.

LEFT: Cast in the shadow of Chevrolet, GMC pick-ups always played bridesmaid to Chevy's bride, but serious truck buyers who were willing to pay a little more for GMC extras came out on top with a more desirable truck.

ABOVE: The 1996 GMC Sonoma SLS features automatic daytime running lamps, a tuned suspension system, four-wheel ABS, and a number of Vortec V-6 engines to choose from. The SLS also comes in a Sportside club coupe model and with four-wheel drive.

The top trim package, the Sonoma SLE, offered a special version with four-wheel-drive and Highrider options that included a wider frame and Bilstein shocks. A driver's-side airbag and lumbar seats to make the long hauls more comfortable could also be added.

Prices range from $10,800 to $24,000, depending on the choice of a 6.1- or 7.4-foot (1.8 or 2.2m) bed. Curbside weight is 2,946 pounds (1,337kg), with a maximum towing capacity of 6,000 pounds (2,724kg) and maximum payload capacity of 1,743 pounds (791kg).

Despite being overshadowed in publicity by Chevy's C/K Series, GMC's success as a truck line should not be underestimated. In fact, the combined overall sales of the GMC and Chevy C/K light-duty trucks during the mid-1990s topped that of the Ford F-Series. Furthermore, the Sierra accounted for nearly half of the overall truck sales in the GMC truck family during that period.

CAMEO

Charles M. "Chuck" Jordan was a pick-up truck man from way back, and it wasn't uncommon for him to be found sketching new designs in his spare time. One problem in particular that Jordan hoped to solve was how to integrate the truck's cab with its bed, thus eliminating that wide gap between the two. Jordan also had a fascination with futuristic vehicles and saw a way to combine his impulses to sketch forward-looking vehicles with practical applications and solutions.

In the early 1950s Jordan was stationed at Cape Canaveral as a young air force lieutenant. He had worked for three years for General Motors in advanced styling before joining the air force. As often happened during his downtime, he found himself doodling futuristic trucks, many of which were illustrated with missiles in the background. He ultimately became partial to a design that would take the utility lightweight truck off the farm and into the city.

Ford had virtually revolutionized light-duty pick-up design with its F-100 in 1953. When Jordan finished his stint in the air force, he returned to General Motors to join GM's chief engineer, Ed Cole, and E. J. Jim Premo, assistant chief engineer in charge of body design, to find a response to Ford.

What emerged was the Cameo Carrier, touted by Chevy as "the newest, most glamorous truck on wheels" from 1955 through 1958. The styling of the Cameo Carrier resembled Chevy's 1955 passenger-car line, which the American buyer had received enthusiastically. The new pick-up featured a wraparound windshield and rear window, a grille inspired by Ferrari, and stylish hood headlamps.

The fiberglass-skinned bed, however, offered the real innovation that distinguished the Cameo from its competitors. In a first attack on his old quandary, Jordan also designed a decorative vertical chrome strip to hide the gap between the slab-sided box and cab. The feature helped continue the truck's character line from the front fenders and doors all the way to the tail of the bed.

The Cameo made its debut on March 25, 1955. Jordan won only a partial victory. Chevrolet/GM officials liked the slab-sided concept, but when Jordan sought to have the bed and cab fully integrated, GM engineers rejected the idea. They feared that torsional flex problems with heavy loads on rough roads would damage the frame and body. Still, the chrome

The 1957 Chevrolet Cameo pick-up sports a heavier grille than its predecessor, opposite. With each year, Chevy added more chrome and options, but not enough to make the truck look overloaded with too many goodies, a problem that the auto maker's car line suffered.

strip at least masked the unsightly gap.

As disappointed as Jordan must have been, his dream was realized in 1959 with the introduction of the single-body El Camino, the passenger car/truck combination.

Uncharacteristically, GM wasn't immediately concerned with turning a profit on the Cameo. The auto and truck maker wanted to test the market for a luxury pick-up truck, and profits were secondary to immediate public reaction.

Some models came with a six-cylinder, 235½-ci engine, and a basic package, but most Cameos were shipped to dealers loaded with options. The dealers actually faced a stiff task in selling these prizes; the Cameos were also equipped with a price tag of over $3,000. Buyers often walked out of the showroom highly impressed with the Cameo, but ultimately they were still walking away. After all, a buyer could easily plunk down $1,500 for a Chevy Big Window Cab pick-up.

Accordingly, Cameo truck production was limited compared with Chevrolet's other truck offerings. Still, more than 10,000 trucks were sold during the four-year period, indicating that the buying public believed they were getting their money's worth.

Despite the flashy styling, the Cameo was basically the same as the Stepside version except for the fiberglass pan-

els. The fiberglass side panels, manufactured by Moulded Fiberglass Company of Ashtabula, Ohio, followed the contours of the cab. The first two model years saw the beds with clean, plain sides. By 1957 the beds sported cast and stainless trim on the sides with a bow-tie insert and Cameo script. The 1958 model also featured identical trim. The taillights, a departure from standard Chevrolet fare, capped the rear fenders for an integrated look.

The fiberglass box did offer two unique features: a tailgate panel and a hidden spare-tire compartment. The tailgate panel, also constructed of fiberglass, hid the steel gate, hinges, latches, and restraining cable. The spare tire was tucked away under the endgate in a

fiberglass well, and was revealed by swinging down the center of the rear fender. Many drivers considered the location inconvenient, however, given the time-consuming task of unbolting a portion of the bumper to reach the spare.

The bed measured 78 inches (198cm) long and 48 inches (122cm) wide on a 114-inch (289.5cm) wheelbase, similar to other short-box '55 Chevy trucks. Five crossmembers provided a wider full-parallel frame for the 3000-Series chassis; these replaced the tapered frame with four crossmembers of the 1954 trucks. Longer leaf springs in both the front and rear gave an easier ride.

Scooped-out trim molding on the fender sides carried the series identification for the first time in 1957, and added a splash of chrome.

Only limited color schemes were produced for 1955 models, including Bombay Ivory and Commercial Red. A year later, eight color combinations were made available. By 1957 the color selections grew to eleven, then fourteen by 1958.

Hubcaps for the 1955 models were taken from the '55 passenger cars, in keeping with the overall Chevrolet theme. The 1956 models used full disc hubcaps off the passenger car of the same year. The 1957 and 1958 versions graduated to their own stylish hubcaps, which were full chrome with trim rings.

Minor face-lift changes came in 1956, with a large "V" added below the Chevrolet logo to distinguish V-8 models from other trucks. Chrome wings extended from the bottom of the centerpiece with the Chevrolet bow tie on the hood emblem. The fender nameplate, newly moved from below to above the feature line, received an additional raised blade.

Inside door panels were ribbed on their bottom half, with a thick, upholstered stripped panel on top.

The 1956 Cameo featured the traditional egg-crate grille common on mid-'50s Chevrolet offers. Note the plain appearance, compared with the 1957 model.

Colors were coordinated with the exterior, and the door sills were wide. Bright metalwork trimmed the windows on the outside.

On the dashboard, the wedge-shaped gauge cluster featured temperature, ammeter, oil, and gas gauges above the speedometer in an unusual configuration that was both innovative and quite pretty. Underneath sat the light, throttle, lighter, and air vent knobs. The dome light hung above the rear window, while the radio speaker was mounted above the windshield, between the sun visors.

Chevy offered basic sixes and V-8 powerplants at that time. The six-cylinder, 235.5-ci Thriftmaster produced 123 horsepower, but an optional V-8 265-ci Trademaster with 145 horsepower came in most Cameos. In late 1956 the maker came out with the Super Turbo Fire version V-8 with 265 cubic inches at 204 horsepower. With the 1957 models, the 235.5-ci six-cylinder engine was boosted to 140 horsepower with the 265-ci pushed to 155. A V-8 283.5-ci at 160 horsepower also was offered.

Customers had a choice of a three-speed manual transmission, a three-speed with overdrive, a four-speed manual, or the four-speed Hydramatic.

Cameo's cousin, the 1955 GMC Suburban, was a marketing effort by GMC to have its own luxury pickup truck. Only 300 copies of this little-known truck were manufactured. Like the Cameo, it possessed a fiberglass cargo box. If one thought the Cameo was the top of the luxury truck market, the GMC Suburban was even flashier. Rounded gauges clustered against the chrome-bedecked dash. The GMC grille was much

OPPOSITE: The two-tone paint scheme, heavy chrome grille and bumper, and quad headlamps on this 1958 Cameo are a dramatic departure from the first Cameos to hit the road in 1955.

larger and bolder than the Chevy version, resembling the 1946–48 Oldsmobile with the massive bomb-shaped bumper guards more commonly found on Cadillacs. The Suburban was a bit longer than the Cameo, by about 4.4 inches (11cm), and weighed about 130 pounds (59kg) more. It was powered by either a 248.5-ci, six-cylinder engine or a rather impressive 287.5-ci Pontiac V-8.

While the Cameo—and to a much lesser extent the GMC Suburban—set the stage for a fleet of luxury trucks to hit the market for the next three decades, its demise was inevitable. The Cameo proved expensive to produce, and the correspondingly high price curbed sales. Furthermore, because the Cameo demanded the installation of the bolt-on fiberglass sides, rear bumper, and tailgate assembly, the car was judged to

BELOW, LEFT: Wheel covers and wide whitewall tires are an option on this '56 Cameo. BELOW, RIGHT: The cab interior differs little from the standard truck offerings in Chevrolet's other truck line.

be labor-intensive. In the end its very existence was no longer cost-effective.

Its initial year saw decent sales of 5,220 units, but production plummeted the following year to 1,452. In 1957 a modest face-lift and more color combinations helped hike sales to 2,244 trucks. By 1958 sales again fell to 1,405. While many enthusiasts argue that high costs signaled the end of production for the Cameo, the introduction of the Fleetside also hastened its demise.

The Fleetside would become General Motors' biggest seller. While the Fleetside exceeded all expectations, the Cameo's role in the future of truck design was never dimished. Without the revolutionary Cameo, a whole new concept of light-duty trucks may have not been realized.

CHAPTER THREE

CHEVROLET

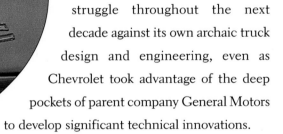

Today it is hard to imagine a truck market without Chevrolet's presence. Chevy emerged as one of the key players in truck manufacturing during the volatile days preceding World War I. The company's initial offering, a 1-ton (908kg) model on a 125-inch (317.5cm) wheelbase, sold in 1918 for $585 without the bed. The next year's model added pneumatic tires, a dry-plate clutch, and three-speed transmission.

The Columbia Body Co. of Columbia, Pennsylvania, was one of several body builders to supply Chevrolet with its panel delivery-style trucks for the 490-Series light-commercial chassis. Rear space for the delivery models was 43 inches (109cm) wide, 56 inches (142cm) high, and 54 inches (137cm) long. Other options included double rear doors and a tailgate with a screen door.

These early trucks competed gamely but fruitlessly against rival Ford's cheap, reliable, and hugely popular Model T car and Model T truck. Still, Chevrolet's dogged persistence through those years paid off. Industry leader Ford would

ABOVE: Rally flags adorning the 1959 Chevrolet El Camino. OPPOSITE: An unusual convertible 1930 Chevrolet roadster pick-up truck. By the mid-1920s Chevrolet was gaining on Ford in the truck sales wars with fluid design, while the styling of Ford trucks remained virtually unchanged for more than a decade.

struggle throughout the next decade against its own archaic truck design and engineering, even as Chevrolet took advantage of the deep pockets of parent company General Motors to develop significant technical innovations.

The Model G ¾-ton (681kg) model debuted in 1921. For this model, Chevrolet's tried-and-true 490-Series running gear and engine had simply been fitted onto a larger and stiffer frame and rear axle. Remember, the Chevrolets of this time came equipped only with cowl and chassis. The buyer then commissioned suppliers like Columbia and other coachbuilders to produce the bodies.

In 1925 Chevrolet brought out its Series M 1-ton (908kg) commercial chassis, a transitional truck that served only until the Series R came out later in the year. The Series R was a handsome, durable machine placed on a 124-inch (315cm) wheelbase. By 1928 Chevrolet had secured a strong toehold in truck sales, challenging the Ford Motor Company for the first time. In fact, that year Chevrolet would annihilate Ford in total new truck registrations, with 133,682, versus

ABOVE: The speedometer of a 1941 Chevrolet pick-up. **LEFT:** The 1941 Chevrolet ½-ton pick-up displays a functional design typical of prewar trucks. Bug-eye headlamps with parking lamps mounted on top give the truck a somewhat streamlined appearance, compared with its 1930s predecessors. Note the push-out windshield for ventilation, and standard painted bumpers.

Ford's 65,247. But it was a short-lived sales victory. In 1928, Ford's restyled Model A cars and trucks reclaimed many of Chevy's recent converts.

The battle for new commercial vehicle registrations saw no clear winner through much of the 1920s and early 1930s. By the late 1930s, however, Chevrolet pulled ahead with more stylish trucks. It would be years before Ford would even come close to matching Chevrolet's overall truck sales.

Chevrolet's lineup in the 1930s included several innovative models. The new Sedan Delivery model, which would remain in production through 1960, featured National Service running gear and special Fisher bodies. This package signaled the demise of the practice of farming out body installation to independent coachbuilders; Fisher was now a division of General Motors. Traveling salesmen preferred the Roadster pickup. This model was basically a sedan with a steel box installed in the rear trunk area.

The 1934 crop of new trucks featured all-new styling, although the careful observer might have noted that the radiator, shell, grille, front fenders, and headlamps looked identical to those of the 1932 passenger cars. Hoods on Chevy trucks were different, though, with louvers on the sides rather than the ports used on the cars.

The CB-Series ¹/₂-ton (454kg) model offered an optional four-speed transmission. Larger trucks were built on wheelbases ranging from 131 to 157 inches (333 to 399cm).

The sharing of the passenger-car characteristics was a stroke of genius for Chevrolet brass, giving the public a vehicle that looks similar to a passenger car but behaves like a work-horse. New truck registrations hit 99,600 in 1933, one of the worst years of the Depression. By contrast, Ford recorded 62,397 registrations, and Dodge scratched out a distant third, with only 28,034 units registered.

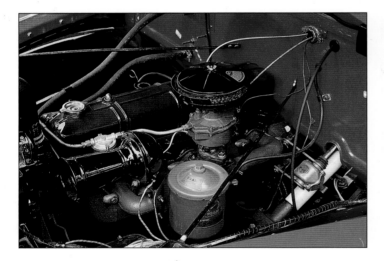

ABOVE: With its modest strength and durability, the 216-cubic-inch Chevrolet Six proved to be the workhorse powerplant for Chevy in both passenger cars and trucks for years to come. RIGHT: This Chevrolet pick-up is a dramatic departure from the auto maker's passenger car line, as a new body style was introduced for the 1955 model year. A chrome grille, wide whitewalls, and dual rearview mirrors were options, painted bumpers, standard.

LEFT: Whitewalls, a side-mount spare, and chrome bumper give this 1949 Chevrolet ¹/₂-ton a handsome look. BELOW: A 235-cubic-inch Thriftmaster engine from a '55 Chevy pick-up.

OPPOSITE: Sales soared with postwar Chevrolet trucks with all-new exterior styling, headlamps integrated into round fenders, and a much larger cab. The five horizontal bars on the grille would soon become a trade-mark for all Chevrolet trucks. This blue beauty is a 1950 model.

The year 1934 brought another batch of radical designs. Instead of the same sheet metal as passenger cars, the ¹/₂-ton (454kg) models now came with their own chrome grilles and headlamps. These models sat on a 112-inch (284.5cm) wheelbase.

Such periodic face-lifts marked Chevrolet's improvement in the light-duty truck field until the dawn of World War II. Even with the outbreak of war, Chevrolet continued building a series of ¹/₂- to 1¹/₂-ton (454 to 1,362kg) pick-ups for military use. One truck model was the AK Series, a ¹/₂-ton (454kg) pick-up used primarily for Stateside garrison duty. As early as June 1944, the War Production Board allowed manufacture to resume on a small number of ¹/₂-ton (454kg) pick-ups, even if only for high-priority civilians.

Chevrolet's 1946 model trucks shared one trait with their rivals: they were all essentially warmed-over versions of models from 1942. For the most part, chrome was still not available on '46 models, due to wartime shortages. Instead, grilles and bumpers were painted to match the body color. Still, it took Chevrolet only one year after the war to reach

LEFT: The 1958 Apache Fleetside offered a full-width body and smooth styling, a departure from the traditional rounded fenders and narrow bed. Load space for the Fleetside was 78 inches (2m) long and 75 inches (1.91m) wide. RIGHT: The dashboard of a 1958 Chevrolet Apache, in a unique two-tone black-and-red paint scheme.

prewar production levels: 171,168 new Chevy trucks were registered in 1946; 1947 saw 235,803 registrations.

In a surprising move for the 1948 model year, Chevrolet continued to rely on prewar designs for its cars, but completely redesigned its truck line. These trucks held no surprises under the hood. The engine remained the reliable Chevrolet Six with a 216-cubic-inch displacement. Heavy-duty models were equipped with the 235-ci, six-cylinder engine that produced 93 horsepower.

RIGHT: The rear taillamps typified the influence of rocket design on this '58 Apache.
FOLLOWING PAGES: This pristine two-tone blue-and-white 1961 Chevrolet Apache features quad headlamps, chromed grille and bumpers, and turn indicators housed in eyebrows on the hood. The Apache was Chevrolet's strongest line.

LEFT: A spacious but spartan interior typical of 1960s offerings in this '63 Chevrolet C-10 offers a full instrument panel in front of the driver with radio and heater controls located in the center. Most truck owners today would kill for a glove-box the size of this one. BELOW: Power, between the 1961 and '66 models, steadily climbed for Chevy trucks. This engine is from a 1963 model.

These vehicles were instead remarkable for their exterior styling. The headlamps were integrated in rounded fenders. The cab was made larger and more rounded than the prewar models. The windshield remained in two pieces but no longer opened, and the wiper was now mounted on the cowl instead of the roof. Even more dramatic was the change to the grille. With its five heavy horizontal bars, this new grille would become the trademark and most distinctive feature of Chevrolet's trucks until 1955, when the egg-crate grille debuted.

The ¹/₂-ton (454kg) model featured a 116-inch (295cm) wheelbase with a 78-inch (198cm) -long bed, which was also widened from 48 to 50 inches (122 to 127cm). This basic truck would remain until 1955, the only exception occurring in 1954 with a new, heavier grille.

Although Chevrolet lagged two years behind Ford in its new truck styling, 1955 witnessed the introduction of several fine Chevrolet design innovations. The new fenders flowed into the door contours, "eyebrow" headlamps recessed into the fenders, a wraparound windshield glinted above the new hood, and the egg-crate grille cut through the air.

Trucks came with only six-cylinder engines early in the model year, but horsepower was boosted to 112 at 3700 rpm for

RIGHT: Perhaps not as pretty as early '60s Apaches, this C-10 Stepside nonetheless remained an inexpensive and low-maintenance mule for small businesses and farms.

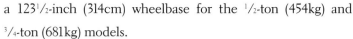

a 123½-inch (314cm) wheelbase for the ½-ton (454kg) and ¾-ton (681kg) models.

Between 1960 and 1966, the Chevy Fleetside and Stepside trucks remained virtually unchanged, although each model year did bring a steady climb in power under the hood. In 1967 an all-new design debuted with a sharper, leaner, and much cleaner look. Buyers could also choose between larger engines, including the Detroit and Cummins diesels. Total truck production for Chevrolet dropped by 72,000 units from 1966, but Chevy still captured about one-third of the total truck market, with 549,665 units sold.

Between 1968 and 1972 Chevrolet held on strong in the truck market. Its new C-10 Fleetside was available in 115- and 122-inch (292 and 310cm) wheelbases and was priced from $2,370 to $2,410. The Fleetside could handle the massive 396-cubic-inch TurboJet V-8 engine, making it one of the fastest production trucks in the country. Excepting annual grille modifications, the Fleetside and the lower-priced Stepside would remain basically unchanged until 1973.

The debut of the 1973 C-10 was a bit of a comedown after the sharp looks of the 1968–72 models. The new C-10 was

the Thriftmaster engine, to 110 at 3600 rpm for the Loadmaster, and to an impressive 135 at 4000 rpm for the Jobmaster. V-8 engines were available only on the Sedan Delivery models early in the model year, but in March 1955 V-8s became an option for trucks.

The Cameo Carrier, Chevrolet's so-called luxury pick-up, debuted in March 1955. Sitting on a 114-inch (289.5cm) wheelbase, its distinctive cab sported a wraparound rear window, chrome grille and bumpers, and a unique, full-width fiberglass bed that easily flowed into the cab contours. While not a practical truck, it proved to be an excellent marketing tool, drawing flocks of new truck buyers to the showroom. The entire Cameo line receives its own discussion on page 46.

By 1955, Chevrolet far outstripped Ford in overall truck sales. New truck registrations for Chevrolet that year hit 329,791, compared with Ford's 295,900. The most popular of the '55 line was the 3100-Series V-8 model, which weighed 3,125 pounds (1,419kg) and sold for $1,519.

For the next year's model, Chevy designers tinkered with the grille design, which was changed again in 1957. Another model with a full-width bed, the Apache, debuted in 1958 with

OPPOSITE: A newly designed grille and less windshield space mark the few differences between this 1966 C-10 and the '63 models. Fleetside models cost a bit more than the Stepsides. ABOVE: A plush bench seat, a horn ring on the steering wheel, and a highly modified dashboard were significant changes in the cab of the 1966 C-10 from previous model years. RIGHT: A 1966 C-10 Chevy V-8 engine.

FOLLOWING PAGES: The 1968–72 Chevrolet C-10 Fleetsides remained virtually unchanged over the four-year span with the exception of grille modifications. But these trucks were by far the most popular on the road at the time, with their no-nonsense styling and wide variety of powerplant options.

softer, a little rounder at the edges, and a bit on the fat side. The 1973 C-10 featured a 6½-foot (2m) bed, weighed 3,741 pounds (1,698kg), and was powered by a standard 307-cubic-inch V-8 engine.

The 1973 C-10's counterpart in the Chevrolet line was the new Chevy Luv (Light Utility Vehicle) mini pick-up. Manufactured in Japan, the Luv pick-up was not considered a true Chevrolet by purists, but it met with great success on the sales floor.

The Luv was Chevy's answer to the Ford Courier, which was introduced in mid-1972. Placed on a 102½-inch (260cm) wheelbase and weighing 2,450 pounds (1,112kg), the Luv featured a four-cylinder 110.8-ci engine. By 1979 the Luv came with a four-wheel-drive option and a Mikado trim package at a price of $4,486. The standard two-wheel-drive version was priced at $4,276. The basic 110.8-ci engine put out 74 horsepower at 5000 rpm.

By 1983 Chevrolet had produced 18.5 million pick-up trucks since it introduced its Fleetside model in 1955, with an estimated 11 million still tooling the highways. The C-10 Fleetside remained the favorite among urban buyers, while the Stepside offered a variety of packages at lower prices. In all, Chevy offered fifteen full-size pick-ups in three series.

The S-Series mini pick-up is touted by General Motors as having the greatest longevity of any full-line light-duty truck put on the road from 1986 to 1995. Sleek, with a rounded nose and strong horizontal chrome grille, the 1997 Chevy S-10 two-wheel-drive pick-up with regular cab and short box is a testament to just how far automotive technology has advanced in

BELOW: C/K engines, like this one from a 1993 1500 pick-up, range from the 4.3-liter, 200-horsepower V-6 to the 6.4-liter turbo-diesel V-8.

OPPOSITE: The 1994 Chevrolet 2500 Club Cab 4×4 comes with an optional 6.4-liter turbo diesel engine that generates 180 horsepower or the 7.4-liter V-8 for 290 horsepower.

the last two decades. The S-10 is powered by a spirited 118-horsepower, 2.2-liter engine with its first scheduled tune-up at 100,000 miles (160,900km) and its first coolant change at 150,000 miles (241,350km).

Also in the S-Series line are the extended-cab pick-up with optional third door; the Sportside pick-up with a bold street package; the two-wheel-drive SS or sport pick-up powered by a meaty 180-horsepower V-6; and the 4×4 ZR2 with bit 31- by 10½-inch (79 by 27cm) tires on aluminum wheels, reinforced wide-stance chassis, and gas-charged monotube shock absorbers.

Three engine options are available for the S-Series trucks. The basic 2.2-liter generates 118 horsepower at 5200 rpm. The heftier 4.3-liter V-6 offers 175 horsepower for the two-wheel drive and 180 or 190 horsepower for the 4×4 model. Buyers choose between two transmissions: a five-speed overdrive manual transmission or an electronically controlled, four-speed overdrive automatic.

Like its mini pick-up brother, the C/K Series has enjoyed lasting durability on the road and rivals Ford in high resale value for 1988–96 trucks. Produced in four models, the C/K Series offers a standard cab or an extended cab with optional custom leather seating and a rear seatback that folds down to accommodate extra cargo. The C/K 3500 1-ton (908kg) model comes decked out with "Big Dooley" dual rear wheels on the extended-cab versions.

A variety of powertrains, ranging from the 4.3-liter, 200-horsepower V-6 model to the 6.5-liter turbo-diesel V-8 with 180 horsepower and the 7.4-liter, 290 horsepower V-8, makes the C/K perhaps one of the most versatile trucks on the road.

Many carmakers pursued a hybrid that would mix the best features of a truck and of a car. Studebaker, Hudson, and even Diamond T tried, but with little success. Later, when Chevrolet decided to go for the urban crowd with the luxuriously appointed Cameo Carrier, the end result proved more of a marketing tool than a practical workhorse.

Thus there was understandable skepticism when Chevrolet introduced its El Camino for the 1959 model year. Here was a vehicle that couldn't make up its mind whether it was a car or a truck. It sported all the beautiful lines of the now-classic Impala, but the El Camino's bed made it a natural for the farm or warehouse. If anything, its biggest downside was the reluctance of owners to dirty it up with a ton of manure or a load of ceramic tile.

The 1959 El Camino took its cue from the sporty Impala, and is perhaps the first passenger car/pick-up truck combination to really work. Too pretty to muss up with heavy farm or ranch work, it attracted urban buyers who wanted something snazzy and masculine.

The El Camino was designed for light-duty work in cities and towns, yet with the option of serving as a reliable and comfortable passenger car. But it would only be offered for two years before being put on hiatus after the 1960 model year.

It could have been a wonderful little experiment by Chevy to see what the market would hold, but General Motors brass had something more in mind. They intended all along to bring the El Camino back, but wanted to ensure that it was based on an appropriate Chevy line that would serve the car/truck well for years to come.

That opportunity came with the 1964 model year. The newly released El Camino retained none of the heavy sheet metal of the 1959–60 models. It was clean and very spartan, yet sleek and ripe for hot-rodding. The 396-ci engine would debut in 1966 to enable the El Camino to become the premier racing pick-up truck of the decade.

The highly practical 1964–67 line of El Caminos is considered to be the forerunner to many of today's pick-ups that emphasize comfort and style. Strong and reliable enough to serve as a pick-up, the payload for the 1964 models rated at 1,200 pounds (545kg) for the six-cylinder models and 1,100 pounds (499kg) for the V-8s.

The '64s also featured air-booster shock absorbers in the rear that allowed the owner to increase the air pressure from any service-station air hose. By increasing the pressure in the shocks from 10 pounds (4.5kg) to as much as 65 pounds (29.5kg), drivers could correspondingly increase the payload capacity. The box measured 78½ inches (199cm) long and 59¾ inches (152cm) wide through the 1967 versions.

Two styles came with the '64. The Custom El Camino offered extensive chrome moldings on the pick-up box, doors, and windshield, and around the wheel openings, as well as an attractive hood build with windsplit molding. The standard El Camino came with a minimum of chrome and all-vinyl seats; the Custom version offered color-keyed pattern cloth and leather-grain vinyl.

A 194-ci, six-cylinder engine, which originally debuted on the Chevy II in 1962, generated 120 horsepower. A 283-ci V-8 with a two-barrel carburetor

(195 horsepower) could be had; the more popular 327-ci V-8 with four-barrel carb (250 horsepower) was also offered.

Chevy inexplicably restyled its taillamps for the 1966 models, turning the taillamps inward despite pending federal mandate that lights be visible from the side. Still, options for 1966 were plentiful, with a variety of manual and automatic transmissions. The 396-ci V-8, introduced on passenger Chevys in 1965, now became an option for the El Camino. Otherwise, the 1964–67 El Caminos remain virtually unchanged.

Pricier versions for the 1967 models hit the showroom floor with even more options and standard equipment. The 1967 El Camino—a favorite model for modern restoration buffs—was, as the last of its body style, the culmination of the El Camino ethic. It balanced the power of a strong workhorse with a sportiness that attracted younger buyers. The taillamps featured three-piece lenses and wrapped

LEFT: The El Camino resurfaced in 1964 following a three-year absence from the market. This 1965 model, not much different from the '64 models, sports clean lines and functional styling. ABOVE: Federal regulations would soon require vehicles to be equipped with side lamps as a safety measure. That didn't stop Chevrolet from inexplicably turning its rear taillamps inward on the 1966 El Camino.

around the sides of the rear fenders. A vinyl, wood-grained strip stretched between the taillamps and across the tailgate. Head restraints and disc brakes were made available. Air-pollution devices made an appearance on California cars for the first time.

Throughout the 1968 model year El Camino continued to share the Chevelle line with Chevy's passenger cars. The 1968 model, however, set the racing crowd on its ear. The Super Sport—or SS—package debuted in 1968 and featured the 396-ci and later the massive 454-ci V-8 engine. It quickly earned a reputation as a terrific workhorse, but it was among the racing crowd that the El Camino really gained its fame. Although perhaps too light in the rear by practical racing standards—control was always a problem—in the right hands the El Camino was a pure racing menace.

The Super Sport package effectively changed its personality during the 1968–72 model years. Sitting on a 116-inch (295cm) wheelbase, the El Camino

A 327-cubic-inch V-8 from a 1965 El Camino.

The 396-cubic-inch V-8 powered the popular Super Sport package in this 1970 El Camino, perhaps the most popular street machine of any El Camino.

By 1970 El Camino came with several different picks for a huge V-8 engine. Perhaps the most rare is the 400-ci with four-barrel carburetor and 10.25:1 compression ratio to generate 300 horsepower.

In 1970 General Motors lifted its ban on engines of 400 cubic inches or more for intermediate Chevrolets. That year's El Camino sported a 402, but Chevrolet, in an odd move, still marketed the engine as a 396. They hoped to capitalize on the old specs' enduring popularity and name recognition.

The 396 came with a four-barrel carb, 10.25:1 compression ratio, and 350 horsepower. Racheting up the power were a pair of 454-ci V-8s, one with a four-barrel carb and 10.25:1 compression ratio to generate 360 horsepower, while the other offered a special camshaft and 11.25:1 compression ratio to generate 450 horsepower. The 454 would signal its intent at illegal street drags with its low rumble at idle and low speeds, then scream its unbridled baritone when unleashed at a green light. There was no mistaking who had a 454 under the hood and who preferred the soft purr of a 327 or, God forbid, a 283.

In 1971 General Motors made yet another marketing move involving its GMC truck line. This time, it introduced the GMC Sprint, the El Camino's cousin, much like what the GMC Suburban was to the Chevrolet Cameo Carrier.

The purpose behind producing the Sprint was twofold. First, rather than use the Sprint as a promotional gimmick to get buyers onto the showroom floor to purchase other GMC products, GMC brass wanted a light-duty muscle car/truck of their own. Second, GMC wanted to be part of the muscle-car crowd.

Buyers could choose from two different engines: the standard 250-cubic-inch, six-cylinder engine, or the GMC Invader V-8, which featured precision-cast

enjoyed all—if not more—of the Super Sport options found on Chevelle passenger cars, after the options were accentuated to fit El Camino's hybrid design.

Black accents were emphasized on the SS 396; the grille, in fact, was almost totally blacked out. A chrome strip divided the dark lower portion of the body from the contrasting body color above. SS emblems abound-ed, including on the front, rear, and instrument panel above the glove box. SS packages also featured Strato-bucket seats and a console. Collectors looking for an authentic SS El Camino should always beware, though: many counterfeit SS El Caminos ride the road today. Their owners liberally apply SS emblems to their cars and replace the standard V-8s with 396s.

cylinder block and heads, positive crankcase ventilation, and a new rocker valve designed to run on unleaded fuel, a novelty for 1971. Handsomely appointed—like all GMC versions of a Chevrolet vehicle—it boasted two-tone paint schemes, a vinyl top, and generous slabs of chrome. It also featured a heavy application of zinc chromate rust primer to all exposed parts.

Another and perhaps more important element of the GMC Sprint/Chevrolet El Camino relationship

The 1970 SS 396 El Camino is perhaps the most desired Chevy truck for drag racing. The 396-cubic-inch engine generates 350 horsepower thanks to a four-barrel carb and a 10.25:1 compression ratio.

was GMC's lack of participation in the building of the vehicle. Larger trucks had always been designed by GMC's Truck and Coach Division and shipped to dealers of both marques, with either Chevrolet or GMC nameplates, badging, and accessories added on. In this case GMC had little to say about the design, the construction, and ultimately the marketing of the GMC Sprint. It was perhaps the first time that a GMC product was supervised by the Chevrolet division.

Although identical vehicles in every respect, GMC always enjoyed a reputation for quality, tough trucks, while Chevrolet made its name in passenger cars. GMC took great pride in the fact that many buyers preferred it to the El Camino. In 1978, GMC changed the name from Sprint to Caballero. The GMC version ultimately accounts for 10 percent of all El Camino sales.

Nowadays the 1968–72 El Caminos are most popular among buyers, as they offer most amenities that new cars provide today. Additionally, they promise huge muscles not found in either the El Camino's 1964–67 versions or any of today's new cars.

CHAPTER FOUR

INTERNATIONAL

There's something enduring about a truck nicknamed "corn-binder." The classic International ¹/₂-ton (454kg) pick-up deservedly won that honor following decades of farm duty on the back roads of the Midwest.

International Harvester Company (IHC), based in Chicago, Illinois, took great pride in its workhorse reputation. During the 1950s the company bucked styling trends aimed at attracting the urban market, instead producing spartan, tough little farm trucks that could withstand a terrific beating. Even when cushy plastic options were introduced in the late 1960s and early 1970s by Chevrolet and Ford, International resisted the effort to sissify its trucks with such unmasculine features.

Between 1908 and 1962, IHC averaged third place in sales behind Chevrolet and Ford, despite its rather arcane styling. Immediately following World War II, total sales of IHC trucks wobbled between the third and fifth ranks. However, IHC's major competition—independent truck makers Studebaker and White—suffered severe financial setbacks in the 1950s. By 1954 IHC found itself alone in third place. It remained there until 1962.

ABOVE: International Harvester Company logo from a 1912 truck. OPPOSITE: This 1939 International D-Series pick-up is perhaps the most sporty of the alphabet series trucks produced by IHC during the 1930s. D-Series trucks featured pontoon fenders, bold lines that swept back from the grille and along the hood to the cab, and a V-windshield.

The origins of International Harvester date back to 1831, when Cyrus McCormick invented his McCormick reaper. This grew into a lucrative business of selling farm machines to the country's farmers. By 1902 McCormick merged his company with IHC. Truck production began in 1907.

International's engineer, Edward A. Johnston, sought to continue providing mechanical equipment to farmers. He envisioned a motor vehicle that would be acceptable to the farming community. That vehicle came in the form of the "Auto Buggy," a high-wheeled machine powered by a 20-horsepower, two-cylinder, four-cycle, cast-iron, air-cooled gasoline engine and a two-speed planetary transmission. During the first year, one hundred Auto Buggies were produced. By March 1910, the roads were filled with 2,700 IHC trucks.

By 1912, IHC began to officially identify their vehicles as motor trucks. The price tag read $600 for a truck with a curbside weight of 1,600 pounds (726.5kg). Three years later International followed the lead of many other of the world's trucks by imitating the French-made Renault. This was a

dramatic change in International's styling. The new trucks featured a four-cylinder, L-head engine with a three-speed transmission with shaft drives to internal-gear rear axles. The radiator was located behind the engine and covered by a front-opening, Renault-styled hood. These trucks ranged from ³/₄ ton to 2 tons (681 to 1,816kg) and ranged in price from $1,850 to $2,800. The old high-wheelers, which had served IHC so well for eight years, were phased out.

IHC's S Series would serve notice of the company's dominant future in the Midwest. The trucks—labeled "S" for speed-truck because they could top 30 miles per hour (48kph) on the unpaved rural back roads— were affectionately dubbed "Red Babies" because of their small size and bright red finish. Mostly marketed as ¹/₂-ton (454kg) models, the trucks were ungainly little things, with tall roofs and square radiators. First introduced in 1922, about 50,000 units were sold through 1929. These respectable sales were achieved in large part as a result of IHC's decision to establish 170 sales branches throughout the country, a move that solidified International's position behind Chevrolet and Ford. Dodge and GMC would not break IHC's third-place ranking until the 1950s.

During the mid-1930s, in fact, International's skyrocketing sales eclipsed those of all its competitors, with the exception of Chevrolet and Ford. IHC achieved 53,471 total truck registrations in 1935; 71,958 in '36; and 76,174 in '37. By the time the United States entered World War II in December 1941,

BELOW: This 1912 Auto Buggy pick-up truck is fitted with rear bench seats to maximize the number of passengers it can carry. OPPOSITE, TOP: This late-teens International with drum headlamps and no cab is a modified version of the pick-up.

OPPOSITE, BOTTOM: Note the sloped front hood of this World War I-era pick-up truck that was influenced by the French-designed Renault. Pneumatic tires were not available when this pick-up was first manufactured.

International had moved 92,482 units. Dodge puttered behind in fourth place that year with 62,925 total registrations.

Part of IHC's success can be attributed to its carlike styling. While not as clean as Hudson's art-deco Terraplane light-duty pick-up or Studebaker's industrial Coupe-Express, the vehicles of IHC's C-Series were nevertheless among the most beautiful on the road. The genius, however, was that the designs remained simple and conservative enough not to put off the farmer and urban hauler.

Between 1947 and 1949 International was locked into fourth place in overall truck sales. The company took 12.37 percent of the truck market in '47 and 12.18 percent in '48, before dropping to 9.77 percent in 1949.

Based on these heady sales, IHC President J.L. McCaffrey and manager of sales W.K. Perkins felt confident enough to introduce an all-new truck for 1950 with the debut of the L Series. Somewhat tall and angular compared with what was being offered by the Big Three, the L Series featured a one-piece windshield and two-section rear cab windows. The front grille sported nineteen vertical blades tapered at each end and placed above a wide horizontal bar. The IHC emblem sat on the nose of the hood, directly above the grille. Single headlamps were recessed into the fenders, with small rectangular parking lamps mounted directly below.

The R Series followed a year later. These trucks offered two-tone paint schemes, a cleaner grille graced by a single horizontal bar, automatic transmissions, and 12-volt electric

RIGHT: Even in the early 1920s, International pick-up trucks sported a square look, as illustrated by this light-duty model. BELOW: The Shera Trucking Company of Richmond, Indiana uses a Pullman train-mobile to transport a long line of IHC pick-ups.

systems. Available between 1953 and 1955, the R Series came in either a 115- or 127-inch (292 or 322.5cm) wheelbase. Different models included chassis and cab, light-duty pick-up, panel truck, stakebed, Metro line, and school bus. R-Series trucks are probably the most attractive of the 1950s IHC products. Still, sales plummeted in 1954 by 20.9 percent, most likely due to Ford's phenomenally successful introduction of the radical F-100 light-duty truck in 1953.

The S Series, or S-120 basic pick-up truck, submitted a less satisfying design, with bug-eyed headlamps that only enhanced its awkward appearance. By the same token, this line offered a wider range of trucks from which to choose. The ³/₄-ton (681kg) model now offered four-wheel drive, and all trucks were delivered with a 240 Black Diamond engine,

except the ³/₄-ton (681kg) milk delivery, Metro van, and Metro-lite trucks. These models bore a lighter Silver Diamond engine with a 220-cubic-inch displacement.

IHC sales remained healthy for the 1956 calendar year; 137,839 IHC models were produced, accounting for a 5.7 percent jump in sales over 1955. More than 2.6 million Internationals had been produced to that point, with an estimated 1.1 million still rolling on the world's roadways.

When IHC's fiftieth anniversary issue debuted the Model A (A as in anniversary) in 1958, it signaled International's signature style through the rest of the 1950s and 1960s. The designers had shed much of the awkward look that defined earlier models. Chrome options and two-tone paint jobs—specifically gray over pink and gray over yellow—made the

The mid-sixties offerings from International were a long way from the R Series of the early 1950s. While rooflines and hoods remained flat, the front fenders were better integrated into the overall design. Parking lamps for the 1965 ¹/₂-ton (454kg) model 900s were placed below the headlamps. Perhaps most impressive was the passenger-car–like aluminum egg-crate grille with "INTERNATIONAL" emblazoned across the center against a black background. An "IH" emblem also adorned the hood. Overall window space offered panoramic views.

In 1965 International conducted a survey to gauge consumer habits in the truck market. It found that nearly 75 percent of the Scout Model 800s with four-cylinder engines and 5-foot (1.5m) beds had been purchased for nonbusiness use. Eighty-two percent of these trucks were four-wheel drives. International also discovered that consumers traded in a large percentage of sports cars and family station wagons to buy a Scout. Production for the calendar year 1965 achieved an all-time high for Scouts, at 26,962.

In the mid-1970s, International held the fifth-place ranking behind the big names of truck manufacturing: Ford, Chevrolet, Dodge, and GMC. Today, International sells its big rigs as part of a vast foreign operation. Its more than one dozen worldwide centers encompass not only truck building, but farm machinery, heavy construction equipment, and power units.

light-duty models rather handsome in appearance. Revisions included a flatter roof and hood and a full wraparound windshield. Up front, the hood featured a wider air scoop—a feature unique to International—and a large, winged "IH" emblem below it. The front fenders were more squared than in previous generations, with parking lamps set above the headlamps inside fender nacelles.

Options included a chrome front and rear bumper, a deluxe cab interior with foam rubber seats, a dome light, door arm rests, an AM radio, a clock, and a cigar lighter. The Series A-100 and A-102 models retained the Black Diamond inline six-cylinder engine with 220-ci displacement and 112.5 horsepower at 3800 rpm. The 240 Black Diamond engine remained, but an enlarged 264-ci engine also was offered.

By 1965, International had turned its attention to four-cylinder models. The slant-four, a V-8 engine virtually sliced in half, was introduced in 1963, engineered to give buyers savings in gas costs. Its 152-ci displacement generated a modest 93.4 braking horsepower at 4400 rpm.

ABOVE: In the late 1920s this ¹/₂-ton International pick-up was as popular for suburban duties as it was in rural areas. BELOW: Note that the headlamps are mounted on the cowl of this International. OPPOSITE: A 1923 Red Baby made quick work of farm duties in rural America. They were known for their speed and durability on rough roads.

FOLLOWING PAGES: International celebrated its fiftieth birthday in 1958 with this handsome A100 ¹/₂-ton anniversary edition.

TOY TRUCKS

Toy trucks are no longer just child's play. The modern toy truck market encompasses a multimillion-dollar business, with a large percentage of the market focused on adults, almost a natural outgrowth of the truck restoration and customizing fields.

Toy truck collecting began at the end of World War I, and soon commercial and light-duty truck dealers were using toy trucks as a marketing tool to attract buyers. When Dad forked over several hundred dollars for a new light-duty truck, his son got a replica of the real McCoy. Farm tractor dealers who crisscrossed the Midwest looking for buyers often used toy-sized replicas of their products as sales tools.

Toy truck scales range anywhere from 1:16—1 inch (2.5cm) for every 16 inches (40.5cm) of the real version—to 1:25, 1:28, and 1:43 (2.5:63.5, 2.5:71, and 2.5:109cm). As a rule of thumb, the smaller the toy, the fewer details can be incorporated. Toy tractor collectors, for example, prefer a 1:16 (2.5:40.5cm) model because it has moving parts. Many truck models, by contrast, are about 1:25 or 1:43 (2.5:63.5 or 2.5:109cm).

Most trucks collected by enthusiasts are mass-produced by the Ertl Company, Scale Models, Inc., Matchbox, Revell, Monogram, Tonka, and Spec Cast. Ertl, Scale Models, and Spec Cast specialize in toy tractors, but since the early 1990s have begun offering an extensive line of toy trucks and cars.

Mass-produced antique collectibles manufactured by such outfits as Arcade, Hubley, and Vindex command high prices in today's collectible market. Arcade and Hubley in particular, which have been producing toy trucks and tractors since the 1920s, have products that command top dollar.

The Arcade Manufacturing Company was originally founded in 1868 as the Novelty Iron Works by brothers E.H. and Charles Morgan. Building novelties in their Freeport, Illinois, workshop, the Morgans produced cast-iron replicas of storefronts, windmills, and various types of pumps. The company eventually evolved into Arcade, producing a wide variety of novelties in addition to its regular line of corkscrews, coffee mills, and stove pipes.

The Hubley Company, founded in 1894 in Lancaster, Pennsylvania, produced early versions of highway construction equipment toys and would later specialize in fire engine, car, truck, and farm equipment toys.

The Ertl Company, now perhaps the largest manufacturer of toy farm tractors, was founded by Fred Ertl Sr. in the basement of his Dubuque, Iowa home. At the end of World War II he began his small venture making replicas of John Deere tractors

A toy Chevrolet truck, like this SpecCast model, is a popular item for young children and adult collectors.

out of melted-down aluminum and aircraft pistons. He was soon producing as many as five thousand toys a day, and expanded his operation by moving to Dyersville, Iowa in 1959. Today the Ertl Company (now owned by the Victor Comptometer Corporation) employs as many as one thousand people throughout the United States. Other toy truck leaders include Scale Models—founded by Ertl's son Joe—and Spec Cast, both based in Dyersville.

Ertl recently produced a line of fifty different die-cast metal vehicles that allow businesses to put their company logo or slogan on the side for promotional items. Versions include the Ford F-1 "Bonus Built" truck, early 1950s Chevrolet panel and pick-up trucks, and the famous Ford F-100 pickup. All of these trucks are featured in striking two-tone customized paint schemes and company logos. Also offered are 1:32 (2.5:81cm) scale models of the Big Farm Ford F-150 pickup made of die-cast metal and featur-

ing slide-in-stock racks, opening tailgate, and detachable front-blade snowplow. Another Ford F-150, also 1:32 (2.5:81cm) scale, offers a horse trailer with opening tailgate along with two horse figures.

Scale Models continues to produce a quality line of trucks to complement its growing tractor replica line. In 1991 it offered a 1:25 scale (2.5:81cm) 1920s International panel truck coin bank made of die-cast zinc with rubber tires and an authentic International Harvester decal identification located on the side. It was sold through Case International Harvester dealers or could be ordered through Scale Models. A similar version, sold as Scale Models' J.I. Case Heritage series, is also offered. Other trucks include a 1940 Ford panel truck and Mack Bulldog AC tanker rig. Scale Models' Amoco series offers the 1920 International Bank, the Dodge Airflow, and a 1920s-era Sterling tanker bank.

Spec Cast has made a habit of producing some fine-quality piggybank cars and trucks in addition to its toy tractor line. These trucks feature hoods that pop up to reveal a detailed engine compartment. As part of its Liberty Classics line, the company provides a full line of 1940 Ford model vehicles: a panel sedan delivery, a pick-up truck with payload or tonneau cover, a tanker, and the convertible with rumble seat, all in 1:25 (2.5:81cm) scale. These collector toys feature gold chrome accessories and even police and fire department accessories. Company logo imprints are available for businesses.

In 1:16 (2.5:40.5cm) scale, Spec Cast produces a Ford Model A tanker, a 1937 Chevrolet pick-up truck, and the 1955 Chevrolet Sedan Delivery.

Like their predecessors, today's toy manufacturers look to major companies to purchase their truck replicas. In many cases, companies wishing to paste their company logo on the side of a 1940 Ford deliv-

The "Bonus Built" F-1 Ford 1/2-ton pick-up truck.

ery sedan must purchase toys in lots of not less than five hundred. But the toy's value has a tendency to skyrocket on the collector market. Toy truck banks typically sell between $15 and $30 retail, but collectors have seen those prices soar as high as $100, depending on availability, scale, and condition.

Vintage toy trucks manufactured by the likes of Arcade, Hubley, and Vindex are difficult to find and even harder to locate in good condition. A midwestern auction house once offered an Arcade 1930s taxi for the astronomical sum of $8,500. It was painted in two-tone black over yellow and was considered in good condition, despite some scratches from its original child owner. Toys like the taxi, which was in reasonable condition, are best left untouched. If the toy is in poor shape, however, restoration may be the only way to realize its worth.

Restoration of toy trucks and tractors has greatly improved over the years. Painting techniques and the quality of paint have improved. Replacement parts are more readily available and are usually top-quality. Also, toy vehicle restorers are more accessible to the

collector. Many farmers who collect and restore toy trucks and tractors have developed a cottage industry of sorts by restoring collectibles for extra income during downtime in the winter months.

Full restoration of a toy includes undercoating a car, truck, or tractor, installing new rivets and tires, and then applying a final coat of paint. Labor generally runs about $20; when adding in the cost of parts, a collector can expect to spend $50 to $60 on a job for a single toy.

Having a toy restored professionally allows the collector to sell his or her product at a competitive price. Like a real car or truck, a restoration job will make the toy better than when it rolled out of the factory. An assembly-line job gives identical application of paint to every toy with the same overspray and same spots missed. A professional restoration usually provides a better paint job, making the toy easily recognizable as not original.

For the old truck enthusiast in particular, the hobby of collecting and selling vintage toy trucks is a growing trend as the collector looks for another outlet for his or her hobby.

CHAPTER FIVE

STUDEBAKER

Studebaker's long, rich history of truck making begs any number of what-if questions from truck historians. In particular, many truck enthusiasts wonder, what would have happened if Studebaker had abandoned its automobile manufacturing when it was floundering in the late 1950s and had focused instead on building trucks?

Indeed, Studebaker was renowned for building quality—although sometimes underpowered—trucks. Robert Bourke's radical styling on the early 1949 2R Series revolutionized light-duty truck design of the '50s, a wave that Studebaker trucks would ride until their demise in 1963. Later models were no less influential. The 1958 ³/₄-ton (681kg), four-wheel-drive model stunned the trucking industry as well.

But Studebaker hung on to its automobile manufacturing with indifferent quality and modest production numbers that couldn't begin to compete with Detroit's Big Three automakers. Ultimately, this division of resources led to Studebaker's untimely demise.

ABOVE: Optional chrome nameplate for the 3E-Series Studebaker truck.

OPPOSITE: For the 1957 model year Studebaker gave its E-Series trucks a face-lift with a fiberglass grille. The new grille gave it a huskier appearance, and its sharp two-tone styling, as seen in this 3-E1 ¹/₂-ton model Transtar, boosted sales a bit.

Based in South Bend, Indiana, Studebaker was founded by Henry and Clem Studebaker in 1852. They initially built covered wagons, then experimented with automobile designs in the 1890s. They constructed their first car, an electric model, in 1904. A gasoline version was put together on a Garford chassis and introduced a short while later.

By late 1911 Studebaker had made major inroads in light-duty commercial truck building with its ¹/₂-ton (454kg) Flanders 20 trucks. Mounted on a 102-inch (259cm) wheelbase, the truck was powered by a four-cylinder, 154.8-ci engine that produced 20 horsepower. In 1914 the ³/₄-ton (681kg) models were introduced and available as a closed-panel, side-delivery or an open-express, body-delivery. Selling for $1,150, these commercial vehicles boasted a 192.4-cubic-inch four-cylinder engine and sat on a 108¹/₂-inch (275.5cm) wheelbase.

In 1917 Studebaker took a decade-long hiatus from manufacturing light-duty trucks to concentrate on car production. One of its last efforts was the combination passenger/express

brief life span, lasting only until 1939. While Hudson had experimented with these comfortable auto/trucks, the Coupe-Express was in a class by itself.

The Coupe-Express was the only completely new Studebaker to be introduced for 1937. It was really more car than truck, but Studebaker marketed it as a commercial vehicle that would be equal to the task of any competing light-duty pick-up truck. More important was the fact that from 1937 to 1939 it was Studebaker's only offering in the light-duty field.

It was hyped by the company as "a new kind of vehicle that rides the driver and passenger with real comfort and pleasure, yet totes a thousand-pound (454kg) load with ease and speed!" It was equipped with an all-steel cab. The vertical grille featured horizontal chrome strips that, at the top of the hood, stretched back to the cowl. A spare tire was mounted on the right front fender. On the dashboard, the speedometer was laid out horizontally with the gauges mounted below it. It even came equipped with a clock mounted in the glove-box door. By the 1939 model year, the cab was redesigned to integrate the headlamps into the fenders. The grille also was integrated into the fenders with a large "S" emblem mounted atop the hood.

Even with its stylish good looks, the Coupe-Express was little more than a novelty. Buyers were unwilling to prioritize luxury and comfort in their hauling vehicles and continued to buy trucks for performance rather than style. Only about 6,000 Coupe-Expresses were sold during the model's life span. When the M-Series truck was introduced, the Coupe-Express was phased out.

Yet, despite these breakthroughs, Studebaker never garnered more than 1 percent of the total truck market. When the economy showed signs of rebounding in 1937, Studebaker managed only 5,129 new truck registrations. That was, in retrospect, the peak year for the truck maker until the outbreak of World War II.

In 1945 the company got a jump on civilian truck production with the 1-ton (908kg) M15 pick-up truck powered by its Champion passenger-car six-cylinder engine. About 4,000 of these early postwar trucks were built. The M-Series truck was manufactured from 1941 to 1942, then resumed after the

truck, which followed roughly the same dimensions of the 1914–16 models that had enjoyed modest popularity in the United States.

The company didn't resume production of trucks until 1927, when it debuted a series of intercity buses. Light-duty trucks also emerged that year with the "Big Six" Depot Wagon and Panel Express models. Most Studebaker trucks manufactured during this period incorporated the Dictator chassis from its passenger-car line. Studebaker stuck with the panel delivery wagons and offered no pick-ups, although many stakebeds traveled the roads.

The first year following the stock market crash of 1929, Studebaker introduced its S-Series trucks. These machines ranged from $1/2$ ton to 2 tons (454 to 1,816kg) and were driven by 70-horsepower, six-cylinder engines. In 1932 the company acquired the White Motor Company, signaling Studebaker's intention to be a major player in the commercial truck field.

Given its ten-year absence from the truck market and its mere dabbling in light-duty delivery trucks during the 1910s, Studebaker struggled for acceptance in the light-duty field. The company took a bold step forward in this field when it offered the Coupe-Express in 1937. Built on the concept of half-car, half-truck, similar to the latter-day Chevrolet El Camino and Ford Ranchero, the Coupe-Express enjoyed a

A 3R-Series 1954 ½-ton Studebaker truck with a one-piece curved windshield.

war until 1948. The 1945 models, although produced for civilians, featured military-style swing windshields and steel inside door panels. A new model 15A Series, with civilian cabs and a slightly more comfortable interior, debuted in 1947. This featured black fenders and steel disc wheels, although chrome trim was still not available—wartime restrictions were still in effect. In all, 43,196 Studebaker trucks were manufactured for 1946, and a healthy 67,811 in 1947.

Dramatic changes in truck styling occurred for the 1949 model when Robert Bourke designed a light-duty vehicle with a double-wall box and no exterior running boards. The rear of the instrument panel was accessible under the hood instead of under the dashboard.

The 2R Series was lower and sleeker than its M-Series predecessors; the 2R Series had more rounded fenders and an attractive front grille that totally abandoned the prewar styling for cars and trucks. At 55,099, new truck registrations

This is a pristine example of a 1955 3R-Series 1-ton Studebaker truck.

for Studebaker in 1949 were its best ever. Today, the 2R Series is considered perhaps the most attractive postwar light-duty truck.

The basic style of the Studebaker truck would remain throughout the 1950s, with modifications to the grille and dashboard, but not much else. The venerable Commander and Champion flathead six-cylinder engines would serve the line for the rest of the decade.

In late 1949 the Commander engine was enlarged from 226 to 245.6 cubic inches. The 170-ci Champion, which faithfully served Studebaker cars and trucks for more than a decade, saw its horsepower increase from 80 to 85 in 1950.

The 2R Series remained Studebaker's bread-and-butter truck until 1954. That year the 3R Series debuted with its one-piece curved windshield, an ivory-painted grille that enclosed the headlamps, and new rounded instruments. A larger rear window graced the new '55 E-Series trucks with an optional

224-ci V-8 available for the $\frac{1}{2}$-, $\frac{3}{4}$-, and 1-ton (454, 681, and 908kg) trucks. By mid-1955 two-tone models were offered. While the basic truck style remained for the 1957–59 models, the company experimented with a new fiberglass grille lined with three vertical bars.

Unfortunately, Studebaker's days as a major player in the industry were numbered. While Studebaker had broken new ground with its innovative 1949 2R Series, Ford rocked the industry with its 1953 F-100 Series truck. Chevrolet followed with its own dramatic entry, the Stepside, then went a step further with its top-of-the-line 1955 Cameo Carrier.

By the mid-1950s Studebaker was simply no longer the leader in styling. Rather, it faced the monumental task of retooling its trucks for a new design if it wanted to compete with the larger truck manufacturers. Company brass, judging that it wasn't economically feasible to design a new truck,

This 1-ton four-wheel-drive 1958 Studebaker pick-up truck sports a standard six-cylinder engine and is mounted on a 131-inch (332.7cm) wheelbase.

instead opted to introduce the fiberglass grille. The grille was relatively cheap to produce, but it changed the character of the truck. Its three buck teeth gave the 3E-Series trucks, now called Transtars, a heavier, more brutish look. A much larger bumper was installed and the parking lights were moved from below the headlamps to the top of the front fenders. A safety swing-away taillamp was now standard equipment, but customers still had to pay extra for the right taillamp.

Options were plentiful. A 259-ci V-8 replaced the 224-ci version. Power steering was available on the 1-ton (908kg) and bigger trucks. Much to the chagrin of Studebaker purists, indicator, or "idiot," lights replaced the oil pressure and ammeter gauges. A four-wheel-drive version was introduced for the 1958 $\frac{1}{2}$-, $\frac{3}{4}$-, and 1-ton (454, 681, and 908kg) models. Wheelbase size for the Transtar measured 112 inches (284.5cm) with the Transtar's overall length at 185.6 inches (471cm).

Despite Studebaker's effort to keep up with Ford and Chevrolet in truck technology and design, its production numbers dropped dramatically in the late 1950s. Model year production for 1956 was 20,218, but that number dropped to 11,185 in 1957 and only 7,085 in '58.

Studebaker's future remained uncertain. Customers feared that the company—now called Studebaker-Packard after its merger with the luxury marque—was ready to close its doors. Two-tone paint jobs and generous options packages improved sales somewhat, but not enough to ensure a rosy future. Even more ominously, even as sales continued to fall, prices climbed to meet production costs.

The Scotsman 4E-Series line was introduced in mid-1957 as a bare-bones offering to complement the Transtar, but model year production remained stagnant at 7,737 units. The Scotsman came with a flathead six-cylinder engine that generated a modest 185 horsepower. The Scotsman enjoyed not the heavy-duty-looking grille but a modified 2R-Series grille left over from the 1954 models. The Scotsman came with only an inside rearview mirror, although outside mirrors were options. There was no glove-box door, and the bench seat wouldn't even slide. Even the hubcaps and headlamp rims were painted to hold down production costs. The Scotsman turned out to be the lowest-priced pick-up truck in the United States, selling for $1,595.

Looking to attract a more sporty and, perhaps, younger consumer, the Champ was reintroduced as the 5E Series in 1960. As always, cost concerns dominated the design. The cab,

The Champ truck in 1960 adopted the new Lark passenger-car look for its cab, but note that the bed kept the same style since its inception in 1949.

grille, dash, windshield, and doors used Lark sheet metal (taken from its compact passenger-car line introduced in 1959), although the box with its rounded fenders followed the same style used since 1949. It was an attractive addition to the truck and became even more handsome when a new box was introduced in 1961 that eliminated the old-style fenders.

The Champ series was available with one-tone paint schemes only, and trucks 1 ton (908kg) and over continued using the Transtar designs. These early Champs were propelled courtesy of the venerable flathead six-cylinder engine with either 170 or 245 horsepower. The old flatheads were finally dropped in 1961 and a new 170-horsepower, overhead-valve, six-cylinder engine was offered.

Studebaker limped along until 1966; its production of civilian trucks halted on December 27, 1963. Today, the postwar Studebaker truck is a desirable collectible because of its timeless, graceful styling, excellent parts source network, and colorful history.

CUSTOMIZING

Have you ever seen a blown '66 Chevy ½-ton (454kg) pick-up born from three cannibalized pick-ups and sporting an '84 454 block punched out to 468 to go from 0 to 60 miles per hour (96.5kph) in twelve seconds?

How about the granddaddy of all four-wheel drives: a '57 Chevy on a '76 Chevy frame with a fabricated suspension system? Add in custom National Spring leaf springs, lengthened spring hangers, and a wishbone design, and this towering monster has 15 inches (38cm) of rear travel and 10 inches (25.5cm) of front travel. Under the hood a 454-ci engine (of course) generates 706 horsepower.

Members of the custom-truck crowd are a breed apart from the distant and staid restoration and give-me-nothing-but-original rocking-chair folks. Chopped, channeled, and blown, custom trucks are not for the faint of heart but for enthusiasts who want a pick-up truck to not only dazzle the eye but to achieve white-knuckle status on the open road or drag strip.

Truck customizers can be drawn into two distinct camps. On one side dwell those owners who conduct extensive customizing projects for the '40 Fords or '58 Chevy Apaches. These folks wouldn't hesitate a moment to stretch and pull their late-model Dodge Rams into custom conversions. On the other side reside the enthusiasts who find every factory and after-market option, ranging from fiberglass hood scoops to rear pans, bumper caps, and billets. One Los Angeles fellow installed $95,000 worth of extras on a single Chevrolet Suburban.

Unlike classic truck restoration, which returns the vehicle to original factory specs, the customization of a truck is a highly individualized, wide-open

This 1934 Ford street rod reflects the taste of its owner. Custom styling is subjective and highly individual.

Rozzo, who owns Off Road Unlimited of Burbank, California, started his ground-up customization with a 1976 Chevy frame to fit the Chevy's '57 body. John Boubel of Off Road Unlimited fabricated a new suspension to give it a towering lift on monster 39½-inch (100cm) Super Swamper Bogger tires on Weld rims. Dual Pro Comp shocks are installed at each corner. In front, Dana 60 heavy-duty axles with 4.88 gears and Power-Lok labor away, while the back is bolstered by a 14-bolt Chevy rear end with a Detroit Locker and disc-brake conversion kit. A hydraulic-ram-assist power-steering system was built by Lee Manufacturing.

Rozzo's 454 features Ross pistons, Crane roller rockers, a dual 750cfm Holley double-pumper carb, custom headers, Flow master mufflers, and a Mallory fuel pump along with a BDS 6-71 blower. Transmission is a Turbo 400 with a Continental torque converter.

These, of course, are just guys who work with the old stuff.

Late-model Dodge Ram pick-ups have been fodder for custom shops around the country since their introduction in late 1993. Custom Conversions, Inc., of Cleburne, Texas, for example, has customized trucks for nearly thirty years, and specializes in Dodges. The latest trick out of Custom Conversions is stretching a

game. There are few rules to follow, so whatever strikes the owner's fancy can be applied.

Take Jackie Lyons of Phoenix, Arizona, and his 1966 ½-ton (454kg) Chevrolet pick-up. The truck started its life as a tow truck with a basic six-cylinder engine and three-speed transmission. But $40,000 and two and a half years later, only the cab and driver's door remain of what was. Underneath the hood of this lowered, fully custom truck sits hardly a speck of its original components.

Parts from three trucks were used for a ground-up custom restoration of the '66 Chevy. The front end features 15-inch (38cm) front disc brakes (remember, the original came with the archaic drums), Bilstein shocks, and power steering pulled from a 1984 truck. The rear end offers custom four-link suspension, adjustable Koni coil-overs, and a 3.36:1 compression

ABOVE: A chopped and lowered 1938 Willys pick-up. Very little original construction is left of this truck.
RIGHT: Massive power, hardly practical for street driving, is the order of the day for street rods, as evident in this 1938 chopped Ford that sports a 331-cubic-inch Chevrolet engine boasting 600 horsepower.

ratio from the transaxle. Fifteen-inch (38cm) Cadillac disc brakes finish off the braking system. A 16-gallon (60.5L) aluminum gas tank was installed, and the 454 engine was rebuilt with a steel crankshaft, billet rods, an Isky roller cam, and an electronic ignition and distributor. Not to be forgotten are the blower and Holley double-pumper carb, Hooker headers, and Walker mufflers. Top speed? Try 128 miles per hour (206kph). Inside an all-aluminum dash is a full set of Stewart-Warner gauges. Lyons finished off this masterpiece with PPG Deltron white paint, chromed bumpers, wooden slats, and polished stainless steel in the bed.

Maurice Rozzo's '57 4×4 Chevy, built with the same dream, addresses a slightly different crowd: those folks who put their trucks to task in the rough-and-tumble California desert.

standard Dodge Ram into a four-door Ram. The end product is no puny crew cab here, but rather a genuine four-door.

To perform such a drastic conversion, the custom specialists first cut the frame in half. Thirty-seven inches (94cm) of metal are added to the frame, as well as the driveshafts, fuel lines, and anything else that stretches from front to rear. The roof is also extended with fabricated 18-gauge steel and fabricated door posts and door latches. The rear doors, made of fiberglass, are reinforced with steel beams. Owners can expected a sixty-day wait for the conversion, a hefty $12,500 price tag for the job, and a truck that's about 600 pounds (272.5kg) heavier. Most of these big babies are pow-ered by the Cummins turbo diesel or the V-10 engines.

One item does cross over between customization fans and the average buyer: bolt-on running boards. A full 65 to 70 percent of smaller truck and sport utility vehicle buyers, including women, end up investing in this after-market addition.

A variety of interior accessories has evolved over the years: wooden steering wheels, leather seat packages, high-tech audio equipment, and even television and VCR consoles as well as compact disc players. Also popular are moon-roofs, custom wheels and tires, and phantom grilles that cover the headlights.

BELOW: A rear view of this Ford F-250 4×4 displays two-tone paint, aluminum rims, a rollbar, and extended tailpipes. RIGHT: This 1975 Chevy Luv gets rare customizing treatment, from an over-sized engine to racing rims and tires.

Customization isn't for everyone. Extensive custom jobs like those done by Jackie Lyons, whether on a vintage GMC or Chevy or a late-model truck customized with extensive sheet metal and fabrication, require a true truckophile willing to invest some big money.

Still, as the base of truck and sport utility vehicle buyers broadens, now encompassing suburban mothers and rap stars, it seems that most buyers today settle for factory and after-market accessories. With every generation of new buyers, however, customizations live on. Even if a truck never sees the off-road duty for which it was designed, old and new truck enthusiasts will find ways to make their ride distinctly their own.

CHAPTER SIX

DODGE

Dodge has recently reemerged in the light-duty truck field as a leader in styling and performance. Its retro-look Ram and Dakota pick-up trucks—with high hood and rounded fenders—lend the new Dodges a masculine, distinctive look unparalleled by any other truck maker. The trucks themselves are heralded for their ruggedness and durability, with military-type styling and reliable powerplants under the hood.

Brothers and cofounders John and Horace Dodge rolled out their first truck in 1914, starting with a 3.5-liter monoblock engine and a rare 12-volt electrical system on a commercial chassis. The company met with exceptional success during these early years, but both brothers died by the end of 1920, leaving the company's future in question.

Frederick J. Haynes was left to administer Dodge Brothers Inc. Haynes professed a determination not only to carry on the traditions of John and Horace but to modernize their legacy as well. Canny maneuvering by Haynes in 1921 brought the firm of Graham Brothers of Evansville, Indiana to build truck bodies using Dodge engines and chassis.

ABOVE: The Dodge Brothers emblem signifies performance and durability. **OPPOSITE:** Light-duty, prewar trucks did not always follow automobile styling, but starting in 1936 Dodge truck grilles bore many of the same features as its D2 sedans. This 1937 Dodge panel truck is a prime example of the integrated look of truck and automobile.

Dodge, in turn, became the marketing arm for Graham trucks by using the Dodge dealership and parts network.

Three years later, in 1924, Graham relinquished much of its independence. It began to build and sell its trucks exclusively through Dodge dealerships, although still under the Graham trademark. In effect, Graham became the truck division of Dodge.

The partnership did extraordinarily well under the Graham name. Total truck registrations for Graham numbered 42,359 in 1927 and 36,542 in 1928. Graham Brothers trucks shared Dodge truck sheet metal and styling, and were designated as Model As.

In 1926 Graham Brothers sold its interests in the company to Dodge to turn its attention to the new Graham-Paige automobile company. Between 1927 and 1929 Dodge phased out the Graham operation to boost its own line of vans and trucks. By 1930, Dodge was the fourth-best-selling truck maker in the United States.

With a healthy new start in the commercial trucking industry, Dodge followed in the footsteps of Ford and

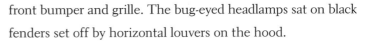

front bumper and grille. The bug-eyed headlamps sat on black fenders set off by horizontal louvers on the hood.

Total Dodge truck registrations closed out at 48,049 in 1939 and hit 62,490 before the bombing of Pearl Harbor on December 7, 1941. During World War II, Dodge built a variety of command cars, ambulances, and personnel and cargo carriers.

When postwar production for Dodge began in March 1946, the company did not offer the popular sedan delivery truck to compete against Chevrolet. Instead, it focused its attention on light-duty pick-ups featuring the same six-cylinder engines found in Dodge passenger cars, combined with three-speed synchromesh gearbox, hypoid rear axle, and semi-elliptic springs. The four-wheel-drive, ³/₄-ton (681kg) Power Wagon was available with a flathead six-cylinder engine, and saw service through 1963.

Body styles for the 1946–48 pick-ups were identical to the 1942 models. The Series-WC ¹/₂-ton (454kg) model rated a gross

Chevrolet with tonnage ratings ranging from ¹/₂ ton to 4 tons (454 to 3,632kg). In 1932, Dodge offered a wide range of handsome trucks with either four- or six-cylinder engines. The 1¹/₂-ton (1,362kg) models offered generous bed dimensions of 99¹/₄ inches (252cm) in length and 45 inches (114cm) wide. Prices ranged from a relatively cheap $525 to $765.

Cab design didn't necessarily follow Dodge's automobile styling, but by 1936 truck grilles closely resembled Dodge's D2 passenger-car designs.

After the Chrysler Corporation absorbed Dodge in 1928, many Plymouth and DeSoto truck offerings paralleled the Dodge line. One such example, the Fargo, was a Chrysler production that mimicked a Dodge in all characteristics except the nameplate. It was marketed exclusively in Canada, although a handful found their way into American hands.

By the close of the 1930s, Dodge was a thriving company, despite the Depression. The Series TC, their lightest truck offering, sold for only $375 for a ¹/₂-ton (454kg) model. A typical light-duty truck featured a modest splash of chrome on the

ABOVE: The six-cylinder engine of a 1937 Dodge truck.
RIGHT: The ram ornament on the hood of a Dodge truck served as a symbol for Dodge products for more than five decades.
OPPOSITE: This 2-ton 1946 Dodge stakebed truck differs little from the 1941 models, as Dodge and other truck makers were not prepared to offer new styling for the first postwar trucks. Early postwar trucks were basically modified 1942 models.

OPPOSITE: The 1947 Dodge 4×4 Power Wagon, converted from military to civilian use, was immensely popular among buyers. All engines were six cylinders and generated 95 horsepower.

ABOVE: This 1954 Dodge ½-ton pickup features an automatic transmission, a rare option. Dodge styling during this period was consistent with other truck makers' offerings, but slightly more square and utilitarian than its competitors.

LEFT: A straight six-cylinder engine powered the '47 Dodge Power Wagon.

vehicle weight (GVW) of up to 4,600 pounds (2,088kg) placed on a 116-inch (295cm) wheelbase with an overall length of 186⅞ inches (475cm). Its bed measured 78⅛ inches (198cm) long by 48¼ inches (122.5cm) wide.

The 1948 model debuted with all-new styling. Its boxy, utilitarian look seems somewhat modest compared with rival offerings from that model year. Nevertheless, in what was a buyer's market, there were 114,431 new Dodge truck registrations for 1948. The year 1951 brought even more ungainly stylistic changes, including a heavier grille and more pronounced headlamps. Fortunately, 1951 also brought several positive additions, including a single-piece windshield and an optional V-8 engine.

Significant improvements came in 1959 with the stylish D-100 and the Sweptside 100. Each of these new trucks exhibited a decent amount of chrome, two-tone paint, a more

LEFT: Unbelievable but true: a pick-up truck with fins. This 1957 Dodge Sweptside took its cue from the Dodge Custom Royal passenger car, which featured flamboyant fins. Here, the fins, with quad rear taillamps, blend nicely with the bed and cab. The squarish front end doesn't exactly mesh with the styling theme of the rest of the vehicle, but it is certainly interesting to look at. OPPOSITE: The styling of the '57 Sweptside bed rivals the Chevrolet Cameo in luxury looks. RIGHT: While many Dodge products in 1957 came with an optional V-8 engine, this model sports the six-cylinder version.

conservative grille, and a flowing beltline that mimicked Dodge's flashier passenger car line.

Under the hood, the Plymouth Valiant, first introduced by the Chrysler Corporation in 1960, bore a significant influence on light-duty Dodge trucks. The Valiant's overhead-valve, slant-six engine was soon installed on ½- and 1-ton (454 and 908kg) Dodge commercial trucks. The slant-six remained on the light-duty Dodges until 1965. The Perkins diesel engine found its way into medium-duty trucks by 1963.

The exterior suffered under less-inspired guidance. In 1961, Dodge rolled out its new flagship Series 100 that only a mother—in this case, the Dodge styling chief—could love. The truck is massively overbodied, with an egg-crate grille that looks too delicate for all that sheet metal. As unexciting as Dodge's styling efforts would be in the next decade, the Model 100 and 200 and the Power Wagon nevertheless enjoyed immense popularity for their handling of tough jobs. Dodge continued with this questionable styling until 1972, although the appearance of the ½-ton (454kg) models improved each year with alterations to the grille and the addition of more sporty options.

In 1972 Dodge went from the case of the uglies to the plain-Jane look. Investing $50 million and four years of planning and engineering, Dodge debuted a clean but unremarkable light-duty pick-up. It featured a more rounded, softer look, a new grille, taillamps, a much larger glass area, and more interior cab room. Engine offerings included the 225-cubic-inch Six, the popular 318-ci V-8, the 360-ci V-8, and a new 400-ci

V-8. A sunroof, sporty wheels, and two-tone paint spruced it up a bit. Servo disc brakes became popular by the late 1970s, and a 4-liter, six-cylinder diesel engine was also introduced.

In an effort to attract younger consumers and custom-truck enthusiasts, trim packages such as Warlock and Macho emerged to provide a sporty look to the line. While the basic design of the 1972 model inspired only the most hardy of Dodge enthusiasts, the company sold more than 1 million units. This basic styling served Dodge into the 1990s.

The restyled Dodge Ram pick-up, first introduced in late 1993, displayed a boldness unprecedented in Dodge's history. This completely restyled truck, clearly modeled on the classic trucks of the 1950s, shook up the industry with its appeal to enthusiasts of unbridled power.

Its style, unmistakably masculine, demands rugged, no-nonsense use. With a raised hood, flared fenders, and a beefy but simple grille (a single vertical bar bisecting a horizontal bar), the Dodge Ram commands attention. Add the optional

V-10, which harkens back to the multicylinder days of the Depression-era luxury cars, and the truck might best be described as an angry beast.

The Ram of the mid-1990s gained instant popularity. Its sticker price ranged from $12,500 to $30,500, depending on the trim and power options. Bed space was offered in either 6½ or 8 feet (2 or 2.4m), with the V-10 engine available only for the extended bed. The Ram sits on a 118^{7}/$_{10}$-inch (301.5cm) short-bed wheelbase, widened to 134^{7}/$_{10}$ or 154^{7}/$_{10}$ inches (342 or 393cm) for the extended versions.

Engine offerings for the Ram include the 5.9-liter V-8 Cummins diesel (175 horsepower at 2500 rpm), the 3.9-liter V-6 (175 at 4800 rpm), the 5.2-liter V-8 (220 at 4400 rpm), the 5.9-liter V-8 (230 at 4000 rpm), and the behemoth 8-liter V-10 (300 at 4000 rpm).

Consider these production numbers before Dodge introduced the restyled Ram: 87,978 in 1990; 80,176 in 1991; 80,098

OPPOSITE: This 1957 Dodge Power Wagon 4×4 is a bare-bones stepside model with no rear bumper and minimal adornments. ABOVE: Most Dodge trucks in the mid-'60s came equipped with six-cylinder engines, but this one, complete with racing stripes and extra chrome trim, comes with a V-8. RIGHT: Interior of the 1965 Dodge pick-up. FOLLOWING PAGES: A Club Cab Ram 2500 four-wheel-drive Dodge Ram is ready for off-road work.

LEFT: Bland styling didn't hinder sales of this 1969 Dodge pick-up, as a variety of power options sent customers flocking to dealers. ABOVE: A customized tailgate, chrome tailpipes, and chrome wheels spruce up this 1978 Dodge Ram 250 stepside. Ram has become a venerable name, synonymous with strength and durability. BELOW: The Ram emblem mounted on the fender of the 250 truck.

in 1992; and 95,542 in 1993. With the first full year of Ram production in 1994, new units skyrocketed to 232,092, then to 271,501 for 1995.

With the redesign of its midsize Dakota in 1997, Dodge dropped the other shoe. Until its redesign, the Dakota had suffered from a severe identity crisis. Dubbed a truck bigger than a mini but smaller than a full-size pick-up, the Dakota was designed to create a midsize truck niche. It met with mixed reaction because most buyers refused to differentiate the grays between full-size and mini.

This new midsize Dakota, relabeled as a compact truck, now serves as a junior version of the good-looking Ram. "Junior" understates its masculine good looks and massive appeal. Bigger than its competitors' mini pick-ups, it uses as many common parts with its big brother as possible, such as identical hood and grille contours, which impart a sturdier, more durable build than other mini and midsize trucks.

LEFT: A ¹/₂-ton 1996 Dodge Ram. RIGHT: The 1994 Dodge Ram, this one a 2500, earned praise from the automotive press for its dramatic styling changes. Somewhat akin to its 1950s ancestors, the Ram is a masculine brute with several power options to choose from. Four-wheel drive is preferred by drivers who use their trucks for heavy-duty work. FOLLOWING PAGES: What worked well for the Ram did just as well for the Dakota. At first considered the poor relation of the Ram, it struggled to find a market. The Dakota has since adopted the same styling as the Ram, with excellent results from truck buyers. This version is a 1997 Dakota Sport. PAGES 116-117: One of Dodge's more unusual offerings during the 1960s and '70s is this 1968 A-100 pickup truck with a van cab. These models were usually powered by a six-cylinder engine, but offered only mediocre road handling qualities. The engine was accessed from an interior panel, between the two seats.

Another plus to the Dakota's construction is that the 4×4 model, for example, shares the same steering box as the Ram, which significantly improves handling. It is even assembled at the same Warren, Michigan, plant as the Ram.

Under its hood the Dakota enjoys considerable power. The 4×4s take either the 3.9-liter V-6 that promises 175 horsepower or the hefty 5.2-liter V-8 at 230 horsepower. Redesigned motor mounts for all Dakotas have minimized engine noise and vibration. To keep manufacturing costs down, Dodge also offered a Club Cab model equipped with only the 6¹/₂-foot (2m) short bed and no stake pockets.

Mopar—a term that includes all Crysler, Dodge, and Plymouth products—enthusiasts anticipate that the Dakota will be considered the premium buy for the mini pick-up truck market. Its size and good gas mileage rank it as a good commuter vehicle. Its price range—from about $18,000 to $27,000—makes it affordable. The Ram and Dakota have also been ripe—much more than their Chevy and Ford counterparts—for customizing, including flashy hoods, grille packages, and even long beds installed on Club Cab models.

Dodge's future is exciting. The company has emerged from the design doldrums to start an industrywide trend. Its pick-ups are more than just legendary workhorses; they are also a fashion statement.

Balzar, John. "The Call of the Pickup Truck." *Los Angeles Times,* September 15, 1996.

Cannon, William A., and Fred K. Fox. *Studebaker: The Complete Story.* Blue Ridge Summit, Pa.: Tab Books Inc., 1981.

Cappell, Pat, and Seth Doulton. "Special Cameo Issue." *Pickups 'n Panels in Print,* February/March 1993.

Dammann, George H. *75 Years of Chevrolet.* Sarasota, Fla.: Crestline Publishing, 1986.

Dean, Paul. "This Ford's Ahead of Its Time." *Los Angeles Times,* December 22, 1996.

"Ford Widens Truck Line." *Chilton's Motor Age,* March 1953.

Georgano, G.N., ed. *The Complete Encyclopedia of Commercial Vehicles.* Osceola, Wis.: Motorbooks International, 1979.

"GMC Announces Changes in 1950 Truck Line." *Power Wagon: The Motor Truck Journal,* January 1950.

McPherson, Thomas A. *The Dodge Story.* Glen Ellyn, Ill.: Crestline Publishing, 1975.

What Every Collector and Investor Should Know About Automobile Restoration. Ontario, Calif.: Batista Automotive, Inc., 1989.